a part of the

QuickStart *series* ™

W. Dean Brown

RAP 411 8909

Distributed in the U.S. and Canada by
Independent Publishers Group
814 North Franklin Street
Chicago, IL 60610
Bookstores and Wholesalers please call 1-800-888-4741

Published by
Consumer Publishing, Inc.
Consumer Corporation
P.O. Box 23830
Concord, TN 37933-1830

Questions please call (423) 671-4858
Orders please call 1-800-677-2462

Consumer Corporation and Consumer Publishing, Inc.
are trademarks of Consumer Corporation.

Designed and written by Dean Brown.
Printed in the United States of America.

The QuickStart Series	ISBN
How to Form a Corporation, LLC or Partnership in California	1-879760-53-3
How to Form a Corporation, LLC or Partnership in Georgia	1-879760-57-6
How to Form a Corporation, LLC or Partnership in Illinois	1-879760-58-4
How to Form a Corporation, LLC or Partnership in New Jersey	1-879760-69-x
How to Form a Corporation, LLC or Partnership in Nevada	1-879760-71-1
How to Form a Corporation, LLC or Partnership in Tennessee	1-879760-76-2
How to Form a Corporation, LLC or Partnership in Texas	1-879760-77-0
How to Form a Corporation, LLC or Partnership in Virginia	1-879760-79-7

Library of Congress Cataloging in Publication Data

CONTENTS

To the Small Business Development Centers and SCORE offices
across the country.

Thank you for telling your clients about our books.

ABOUT THE AUTHOR

Dean Brown graduated with honors from the University of Tennessee in 1985, with a Bachelor of Science Degree in Accounting. After graduation, he worked for the small business services division of Price Waterhouse, one of the largest public accounting firms in the world. Here, the author worked to help small business owners find better ways to operate their business. Working with these small businesses made him aware that they operate on tight budgets.

Unfortunately, no matter how great the benefits of incorporating are, many small business people can't afford to pay a professional to incorporate their business, and most don't know how to do it themselves. To fill this need, a series of how-to-incorporate books was started. Since 1991, Dean has since written over forty books on the subject of starting a business.

He wrote his first book on a borrowed computer, had samples printed up at Kinko's and sent them off to Walden and B. Dalton bookstores. The books were well received and the stores placed orders for almost 300 books. Kinko's duplicated these first 300 books, and Dean bound them by hand on his dining room table.

He makes his home in Knoxville, Tennessee where he writes, operates Consumer Publishing, and occasionally speaks at the University of Tennessee School of Business. He loves working out at the gym, tinkering in the yard, and being in the great outdoors, especially the nearby Great Smoky Mountains National Park. He has a wife Cherie, two daughters Mallory and Amber, and a son William.

Drop me a line!

Starting a business is a wonderful, sometimes scary thing. It's kind of like a roller coaster, a lot of fun, and a little scary. You are off on a fantastic journey, thank you for taking me along. I've made many friends producing these books for the last seven years, some very close. I hope you will be one of them.

If you feel this book has helped you, please drop me a note or a post card of your hometown to let me know. I thoroughly enjoy them. Please send them to:

Dean Brown
Consumer Publishing Inc.
P.O. Box 23830
Concord, TN 37933-1830

Introduction

Before We Go

If you've never started a business before, relax. Forming a corporation, LLC, or partnership is easier than you think. As a matter of fact, if you can put your name and address on a form, you can organize your business. If you're starting a business for the first time, you're probably a little anxious, maybe afraid you'll do something wrong or leave something out, but don't worry, I've worked hard to make this easy for you - you can't do anything wrong. So please, sit back, relax, and spend a couple of hours with me. We'll have your business organized in no time. And by the way, thank you for choosing this book.

In a Hurry?

If you're in a hurry to organize your business and you know a little something about starting one, you can form your business in just a few minutes using the QuickStart instructions. If you want to use QuickStart, read Chapter One, then go straight to Chapter Six and use the instructions to complete the form(s) you need. When you're done, you can come back and read the rest of the book. It contains important information designed to get you started off on the right foot. It'll only take you a couple of hours to read, and will be well worth your investment of time.

This book is thin for a reason - so you can organize your business fast. My goal here is not to give you a law degree, but to sort through the law, digest it, and give you what you need to quickly organize your business and get busy making a living. If you want to further explore any of the subjects in this book, we have additional texts available. Please see the order form at the back of the book or call our office at 1.800.677.2462.

What this book won't do...

This book is designed to help you form a typical business - a basic business partnership, a basic business corporation, C Corporation, S Corporation, close corporation, or limited liability company.

You can form a limited partnership, nonprofit corporation, or professional corporation with this book but the forms will require modifications, some major. If you want to organize one of these types of entities, this book is a good place to start (mainly because it's easier to understand than most) but more specialized texts are available. For information on limited partnerships, nonprofit corporations, or professional corporations, see the order form at the back of the book or call Consumer Publishing at 1.800.677.2462.

How it's organized...

Let me explain how this book is organized. The most important thing you need to know is that we won't discuss specifics until the last chapter. The first few chapters are all general, that is, good for any state. Only the last chapter is specific. I designed the book this way so you can see the "big picture" first, covering the details after we've explored the basics.

Chapter one explains the differences between sole proprietorships, partnerships, corporations, and limited liability companies. This is a very important chapter, one not to be missed. Use it to help you decide which type of business organization is best for you.

The next three chapters have only one subject each. Chapter two covers corporations. Chapter three covers limited liability companies, and chapter four covers partnerships.

The last chapter, chapter six, is the most important. It's the heart of the QuickStart series. It'll show you exactly how to organize your business and includes the forms and QuickStart instructions you'll need.

Libraries...

Many of our books found in libraries are donated. We donate them to help the library and introduce you to our books. If you are borrowing this book from a library, please don't photocopy it. Book sales keep us in business and allow us to continue helping small business owners. Thank you for understanding. This book is available at most bookstores, sometimes found in the "Regional" or "Local" section, and sometimes in the "Business" section. You can also get a copy from us by calling 1.800.677.2462.

Accuracy...

Everything possible to insure the accuracy of this material has been done, but please understand that laws and procedures are constantly changing, and are subject to different interpretations. Since we live in such a litigious society, neither Consumer Publishing Inc., the author, nor anyone associated with this book makes any guarantee or warranty about the information it contains, or questions answered by phone. Also, the state after which this book is entitled is not responsible for its contents. The responsibility of starting and running a business rests with you. Use of this book and related information constitutes your agreement with this disclaimer.

Errors...

If you experience any difficulty, or encounter any changes, please let us know so that we may assist you and keep our books updated. This book is not designed to give legal or tax advice, and the material contained herein should not be viewed as such. If you feel you need the services of a professional, you should seek them.

Forms...

This book was constructed so the pages could be removed easily. The forms are as easily removed from this book as a sheet is torn from a note pad. All you need to do is open the book to the page you wish to remove. Then, while holding that page, open the book as far as possible until the front and back covers are touching each other, and gently pull the form out. If you have difficulty removing any pages, or damage any while removing them, please call us and replacements will be sent immediately. Rather than tear the forms out, most people photocopy them and use the copy.

Forms on disk...

If you want to type the forms on your computer, a computer disk with all the forms is available. The disk is a regular 3.5 inch disk and is available for IBM PC (Windows) and Mac compatible computers. The disk includes all the forms in the book except the IRS forms and works with most word processors.

Call a lawyer...

If you read this book and decide that you need a good lawyer or CPA to help you, here's how to find one. The best way to find good professional help is to ask your friends who they use. If none of your friends own a business, ask the owners of businesses that you patronize. Business owners are a pretty good source of referrals. Also, a good place to find an attorney is the Bar Association in your town. They usually provide a free referral service. You can find them in the white pages of your telephone book. If you live in Atlanta, look under "Atlanta Bar Association Referral Service."

Sole Proprietorship, Partnership, Corporation or LLC

Which Is Right For You?

One of the first executive decisions you'll make for your new business is deciding how to organize it. Basically, there are four different ways to organize a business. Listed from the simplest to the more sophisticated they are:

- *The sole proprietorship*
- *The partnership*
- *The corporation*
- *The limited liability company (LLC)*

The choice you make here is important because it will determine what your business can and cannot legally do, what will happen if someone sues you, how your business is taxed and things like that.

You see, a business only exists because a group of lawmakers, a legislature, passed a special set of laws that governs its formation and operation. The type of business organization you choose determines which set of law governs your business, and therefore how it is formed, how it will operate, and what rights it will have. For example, a corporation only exists because your state legislature passed a special set of laws that governs corporations. These laws determine what a person has to do to form a corporation, what the corporation can and cannot do, and how the corporation will be taxed.

The Sole Proprietorship

A sole proprietorship, as the name suggests, is a business with one owner. Of the four types of business organizations, it is probably the most common. A business organized as a sole proprietorship is not separate from its owner, but merely a different name with which the owner represents him/herself to the public. The owner is the business and the business is the owner. They're inseparable.

Advantages...
Since they have few legal requirements, sole proprietorships are easy to form and operate. They can also be more affordable since no legal documents need to be filed in most cases. Basically, all you have to do to form a sole proprietorship is get a business license and begin operations. Needless to say, since there are little or no legal requirements to satisfy when forming a sole proprietorship, it is not covered in this book.

Disadvantages...
Although the sole proprietorship does have the advantage of simplicity, the negative aspects should steer entrepreneurs away from this form of business organization. The disadvantages of a sole proprietorship stem from its very nature - the business and the business owner are inseparable. This leads to three potential problems.

Unlimited liability - Since the owner and the business are inseparable, whoever sues the business actually sues the owner personally. A single lawsuit can financially ruin a sole proprietorship and its owner because the owner's personal property can be taken to satisfy judgements against "the business." The owner's personal exposure is unlimited.

Responsible for business obligations - The business owner is personally liable for the debts of the company, and unfortunately, personal assets like cars, savings, and homes can be taken to pay company obligations.

No tax benefits - Owners can lose some lucrative tax free fringe benefits because they cannot participate in company funded employee benefit plans like medical insurance and retirement plans. Since the owner is the business, he/she cannot be an employee, and therefore can't participate in "employee" benefit plans. (Some owners get around this by hiring their spouse as an employee, and the spouse participates in the employee benefit plans.)

Taxes...
For taxation, since the owner and the business are the same "entity" for tax reporting purposes, a sole proprietorship is known as a pass-through entity. This means that all business income and expenses pass-through to, and are

filed as, part of the owner's personal return. If there is a business loss, the owner will enjoy a deduction to offset personal (paycheck) income. However, if the business makes a profit, the owner is responsible for any taxes due.

The Partnership

A partnership is similar to a sole proprietorship but has two or more owners. Like the sole proprietorship, the partnership is not a separate legal entity from its owners. Like a sole proprietorship, you don't have to file papers with the state to form a partnership, but you should adopt a partnership agreement. A partnership agreement outlines the arrangement between the partners for running the business and dividing the profits. You don't have to adopt a partnership agreement, but doing so will help settle arguments before they begin. We'll learn how to write a partnership agreement in chapter four.

Advantages & disadvantages...
In general, the partnership shares the same advantages and disadvantages as the sole proprietorship. However, the partnership has an additional drawback. A partner can be held liable for the acts of the other partners, increasing personal liability. For example, if Brent and Irene are partners and Brent incurs a debt on behalf of the partnership, Irene is also liable for the debt even if she knows nothing about it.

Taxes...
Tax treatment of the partnership is also slightly different. Although it is a pass-through entity, the partnership does file an "informational" tax return (Form 1065) with the IRS showing its income and expenses. The pro-rata share of partnership profit or loss is shown on each partner's personal return. Any taxes due are paid by the partners on their personal returns. Conversely, if the company loses money, the partners will share a deduction on their personal return.

The Corporation

The corporation was conceived to solve the typical problems of the sole proprietorship and partnership forms of business organization. Incorporating allows a group of entrepreneurs to act as one, much the way a partnership does, with one important advantage. Since the corporation is a separate legal entity capable of being sued, it can protect its owners by absorbing the liability if something goes wrong. (This aspect of the corporation keeps you from losing your house if someone sues the business.) Also, many people incorporate to avoid personal liability for the debts and liabilities of the business. In recent years, the corporation has become a tax reduction and tax planning tool.

There are all sorts of technical explanations of what a corporation is. Here's a textbook definition: *A corporation is a body of persons granted a charter legally recognizing them as a separate entity having its own rights, privileges, and liabilities separate from those of its members.* It is a separate and distinct entity that acts for, or on behalf of a person or group of people. A corporation can consist of one person.

A corporation is "brought to life" when a person, the incorporator, files a form with the state known as the articles of incorporation. You can think of the articles of incorporation as the corporation's birth certificate.

Corporations are created primarily to operate a business for the benefit of its owners-the shareholders. When you incorporate a business, you actually create an "artificial person" and let this "person" operate your business for you, subject to your control. A corporation is essentially a legal "person" created and operated with the permission of the state where it's incorporated. It's a person like you and me, but only "on paper." As a legally recognized person, a corporation enjoys most of the rights and privileges that you and I do. Among other things, a corporation can own property, sue, be sued, and of course, operate a business. Corporations also enjoy many of the privileges enumerated in the Constitution and the Bill of Rights like freedom of speech. The only difference between a real person and a corporation is this - a person has a physical body and a corporation does not.

S Corporations...

An "S" Corporation is the same as any other business corporation with one important difference-the IRS allows it to be taxed like a partnership, making it a pass-through entity.

When business corporations are created, they are all regular "C" corporations. If you want to be an S Corporation, you must file a form with the IRS known as a Form 2553. This form tells the IRS that you want your corporation to be taxed like a partnership - a special filing status. This means that the corporate income or loss at year-end will be filed on your personal return. If your corporation makes money at the end of the year, your personal income will increase. If your corporation loses money at the end of the year, you will enjoy a deduction on your personal return up to the amount that you invested in the company.

Many people begin corporate life as an S Corporation when there are losses to offset their "paycheck" income and then revert to C Corporation status when the corporation begins to make taxable profits. It is important to remember that being an S Corporation is a tax matter only. It is simply a tax filing status like "single" or "married filing jointly" or "head of household."

S Corporation vs C Corporation...

Which is best? Well, everyone's personal tax situation is different, but I prefer operating as a C corporation. Why? Because I don't want my business income and expenses ending up on my personal return like they do with an S Corporation. I want my business income and expenses to stay separate like they do with a C Corporation. You see, if your S Corporation makes a profit at the end of the year, that income ends up on your personal 1040 return increasing your personal income, increasing your personal income taxes. Also, with a C Corporation, you can deduct more medical and dental expenses than you can with an S Corporation, something very important to me. Also, if you own a C Corporation, you can take advantage of "income splitting."

Income splitting is a way to lower your overall tax bill by leaving some of your year-end profits in the corporation, which is then taxed at a lower rate than if you'd paid the tax on your personal 1040 return. Using income splitting helps keep you and the company in a lower tax bracket, saving you money in taxes.

Advantages...

Some people incorporate for one reason. They like to have "Inc." after their business name, and that's okay. They've always wanted to have a company of their own, and if they're going to have a company, they want it to be a corporation - it sounds BIG! In fact, it can sound impressive to customers and suppliers. It can indicate that your business is larger than it actually is, perhaps making customers and suppliers more willing to do business with you.

On a more practical note, the corporation offers benefits to you because of its legal nature. Since a corporation is a separate legal entity, the corporation actually owns and "operates" the business for you. This separation provides a legal distinction between you and your business and thereby provides three important benefits. First, incorporating offers you the protection of limited liability for actions of the corporation; second, you are not responsible for company obligations; and third, incorporating offers some terrific tax breaks.

Limited liability - Since you and your company are now two separate legal entities, lawsuits can be brought against your company instead of you personally. Separating you (the shareholder) from your business offers protection. Since the corporation has the right to sue and be sued, a person bringing a lawsuit will typically sue your corporation instead of you personally. This is usually the case even when the owner is the only shareholder, the only director, and the only officer. For example, if someone sues Ford Motor Company, the person bringing the suit will simply sue Ford Motor Company. Mr. Ford probably won't even be involved.

Please note that this is what typically happens, or at least what should happen. However, sometimes when a person sues your company, they sue everyone associated with the company, anyone near the building, the janitor, and even the President of the United States if they think it will get them some money. Nevertheless, even if you are personally named in a lawsuit, your corporation can handle the lawsuit and still protect your personal property. The key here is to make sure your corporation has proper insurance coverage. The corporate entity won't take the place of insurance and good business practices.

Not responsible for company obligations - When debt is incurred in the company name, you are not personally liable for it and your personal assets cannot be taken to settle the company obligations. Say for example, you lease a computer for your corporation and put it in the company name. Then, at some point down the road the business goes under. The company that leased the computer to your business can't come after you personally for the lease payments. They can only look to the now defunct corporation for the payments. If the corporation has no assets or money in the bank, the creditor will have to be satisfied with the repossessed equipment. The computer company simply extended credit to a corporation that is now out of business. There is no money to collect. The same goes for all your suppliers, the landlord and so on.

It's important to note here that this limitation only applies for debt incurred in the corporate name that you did not personally guarantee. That is, when you incurred the debt or signed the contract, you didn't personally guarantee payment of the obligation in the event the corporation couldn't make the payments. If you personally guaranteed payment of the obligation, the corporation can't do anything to protect you. You'll have to make the payments. That's why it is important to sign your name on a contract as an officer of the corporation. That is, sign like this, "ABC Corporation, by Jane Gray, President.

Tax benefits - Being incorporated allows you, the owner, to hire yourself as an employee (typically as president) and then participate in company funded employee benefit plans. You benefit by receiving these benefits tax-free and the corporation gets a deduction for providing them to you. These tax benefits usually only apply to C corporations because expenses from the S Corporation are reported on your personal return and therefore either reduced or eliminated.

My favorite company provided benefits include retirement plans and medical and dental reimbursement plans. Let me tell you a bit about them. Using a company provided retirement plan or pension plan, your corporation can put away a sizeable amount of money each year for your retirement and deduct the amount from its income as a business expense.

Most everyone is familiar with retirement plans. They are the company sponsored retirement accounts that most large companies offer to their employees. The best thing about a pension plan is that the contributions made to your account by your corporation are tax deductions for the corporation, but are not taxable to you until you retire. These contributions earn interest and multiply with no tax implications to you, while the corporation's tax bill is lowered by thousands of dollars per year. If you have an S Corporation, making these contributions can lower your personal tax bill. It's kind of like an IRA without the small annual limit.

If you operate as a C Corporation, things can be even more lucrative. You can actually borrow money from your retirement account if certain easy to meet requirements are satisfied. Borrowing from your pension fund allows you to use this money now without paying taxes on it.

A medical and dental reimbursement plan is an employee benefit plan that allows your corporation to pay for your insurance premiums, deductibles, and co-payments. The corporation can also reimburse you for expenses you incur for eyeglasses, braces, and so on. (You're probably beginning to see how beneficial a plan like this could be.) You can spend thousands of dollars annually on these items that even the best insurance doesn't pay for. Fortunately, when your business is incorporated, the corporation can pick up the tab for these expensive items. A benefit plan like this can save you thousands of dollars per year and provide the corporation a tax deduction. A medical and dental reimbursement plan is a standard fill in the blank type form available in our corporate outfits or on the computer disk. See the brochure for details.

Please note that since the S Corporation passes its deductions to the shareholder's personal tax return, only a percentage of health insurance premiums are deductible. If you want to take full advantage of having your corporation pay your health care costs, you'll need to operate as a C Corporation.

Disadvantages of incorporating...
The typical disadvantages of incorporating are often listed as increased administrative duties, the high cost of incorporating, the inflexibility of having a separate entity, and "double taxation" none of which are very good arguments against incorporating.

Administrative - The only real administrative duty is holding an annual shareholder meeting, and all you have to do here is use one of our prewritten forms once a year to satisfy the requirement. You may also need to hold a director's meeting to vote on important matters from time to time.

Cost - The cost of incorporating isn't high if you do it yourself. You can put your name and address on a form and send it to the state. Your only cost is the purchase price of this book plus state filing fees.

Inflexibility - The corporate form of operating your business can at times be inflexible, especially if you've previously operated your business as a sole proprietorship. For example, a person operating as a sole proprietorship can co-mingle (mix) his/her personal and business assets. After incorporating, personal and corporate assets must be segregated, and accounted for separately.

Double Taxation - The "double taxation" aspect of corporations only applies in the case of a large dividend-paying corporation like IBM. Double taxation doesn't usually apply to a small corporation. Let me explain. If a corporation pays a cash dividend to its shareholders, the payment is not tax deductible by the corporation. Since the payment is not tax deductible like regular expenses are, the corporation has to pay income tax on the dividend it paid to the shareholders. When the dividend is received by the shareholder, it is then taxable income to him/her. Therefore, tax on the amount of the dividend is paid once by the corporation and then paid again by the shareholder, resulting in double taxation - but hold on. Small corporations never pay dividends, or shouldn't pay dividends. In a small corporation, the owners receive money from the corporation in the form of salaries and bonuses, all of which are tax deductible by the corporation. The amounts are only taxed when received by the shareholders, resulting in no double taxation.

State Taxes - The only real disadvantage of incorporating as I see it is taxation of corporate income by a state government. If a state taxes corporate income, which most do, it can be a problem as your sales increase to the point where you have a profit at the end of the year. When you are starting off, you probably won't have to worry about paying taxes on corporate income, because there won't be any income (profit). Your expenses will usually keep up with sales and leave you with no taxable income at the end of the year. But as your business grows, you will probably begin to have profits at year-end and therefore State and Federal income taxes to pay.

Of course there are ways around this. You can "eat up" a lot of income by giving yourself corporate paid benefits like health insurance and retirement plans. You can also purchase equipment and reduce your income in other ways. Many owners of small companies simply write themselves a bonus check at the end of the year and "zero out" the income of the business by increasing salary expenses. This leaves no income to tax. As a matter of fact, most small businesses are able to reduce their income to zero and incur no income tax. So with a little tax planning, you'll pay no State or Federal income tax and get to enjoy the corporation provided fringe benefits too.

Limited Liability Companies

A limited liability company (LLC) is the newest form of business organization. Although it was conceived as a replacement for the "limited partnership" to be used in real estate financing deals, the LLC is becoming an alternative to the corporation. Available in all 50 states, it's a hybrid entity that provides the limited liability of the corporation with the taxation status of a partnership, making it a pass-through entity. You can look at it like this, the LLC is a "corporation" that's taxed like a partnership. It's very similar to an S Corporation, but the S Corporation can't have more than 75 shareholders. I think of the LLC as an "S Corporation without the 75 shareholder limit."

The Limited Liability Company is a popular type of business entity, but it does have a couple of disadvantages. First, its newness means that law regarding the LLC is still evolving and some issues regarding its operation remain unsettled. Also, if the LLC is taxed as a partnership, business owners will lose company funded benefits and the LLC income will end up on the owners' personal tax returns.

Of The Four Types, Which is Best?

Everyone has a different answer to this question. Every book will have a chart listing the advantages and disadvantages of different types of business entities and tell you to ask your CPA or attorney which is best. I will advise the same, but I realize that not everyone has a CPA or attorney they can consult with, so I will try to direct you further. Bear in mind that everyone's business is different and everyone's tax situation is different. You may want to refer to the chart on page 23 for guidance.

Sole proprietorship...
I only recommend this type of business entity for the person starting a very small, probably part-time business with no employees. This business would have no assets and its product or service would be one of low lawsuit potential. That is, your customers wouldn't be likely to be injured by one of your products. My mother used to make crafts and sell them at local craft fairs. This is the ideal sole proprietorship business. It's usually started just to make a little extra money.

Partnership...
The ideal candidate for this type of business entity would fit the same criteria as the sole proprietorship mentioned before except this business would have more than one owner. Like the sole proprietorship, a partnership can be incorporated or converted into an LLC later on if the business grows beyond its initial expectations.

Corporation...

This type of organization is best suited for a single entrepreneur who wants a small business that offers tax advantages and tax planning capabilities or a group of entrepreneurs who want to start a business that will grow in size and have employees. Its limited liability aspect makes the corporation ideal for companies with products or services with liability potential. In today's litigious society, you need all the protection you can get.

Limited liability company...

This type of business organization is ideally suited to those who want the limited liability protection of the corporation but want to be taxed as a partnership - perfect for real estate investment businesses. Being "taxed as a partnership" means that the business profit or loss ends up on the owner(s) personal return(s), and there are few if any personal fringe benefits.

Many people think that the LLC is best because it is the latest thing. Newer must be better, right? Well, maybe not. The LLC is a good business vehicle for your business, but it may not be the best. It's really just a new twist on an existing type of business organization, a "close" corporation that elects to be taxed as an S Corporation. The close corporation, if available in your state does away with a lot of the administrative requirements of a regular corporation, and choosing S Corporation tax treatment makes it a pass-through entity.

There are only two cases where I'd favor organizing as an LLC over organizing as a corporation; if the company invested in real estate or if the company was formed in a state that taxed corporate income and not LLC income.

Real estate - Since they are taxed like a partnership, LLC losses sometimes generated in the early years offer a tax write-off to the owner, coupled with favorable taxation of the financial rewards at the maturity of the project. Perhaps a perfect fit for those starting a real estate investment business that buys houses, rents them while they appreciate in value, and sells them at some point in the future.

State taxes - If you do business in a state with no personal income tax, *and* no tax on the LLC income, *and* you *don't* want to take advantage of the fringe benefits a corporation offers, the LLC might be for you. In Tennessee for example, there is no tax on personal income and no tax on LLC income. If you live in Tennessee and have no interest in the fringe benefits offered by incorporating, you might choose the LLC if your business is making a profit. This way, you won't have to pay the 6% state income tax on corporate income. If your business doesn't make a profit, the LLC won't save you any money because there's nothing to tax.

Something to think about...

Before you choose a sole proprietorship, a partnership, or LLC, all of which are pass-through entities where your business profits end up on your personal return, let me point something out. Think about this for a minute. Do you realize that if your LLC, sole proprietorship, or partnership makes a profit it will increase your personal income by the amount of the profit? Say for example, your pass-through entity has a really good year and has a profit of 75,000. Do you realize that your personal income on your 1040 return is now the amount that you paid yourself PLUS the $75,000? Now think about this...

Where are you going to get the approximately $25,000 to pay the taxes on this income? Of course, you'll write a personal check for it - pay your "business" taxes with personal funds, personal funds that you've already paid taxes on once - not a good idea.

What if you don't have the $25,000? You'll have to either borrow it, or take it out of the business. Of course if you take it out of the business, you'll have to report it as income on next year's tax return and pay taxes on it - not a good idea. This means that you've increased your personal income and taxes for *next* year just to pay the taxes on business income that ended up on your personal return *this* year. Ouch! The moral of the story? You don't want to be taxed as a pass-through entity if your business is making a profit. It's better to be a C Corporation if you're making a profit.

What I Did

Consumer Publishing started out as an S Corporation. Since I didn't think I'd make a profit with the company for two or three years, I started with the S Corporation because it is taxed like a partnership, a pass-through entity. This allowed me to pass the business losses incurred in the start up period through to my personal return and get a personal tax deduction for losses incurred by the business. The limited deductions available to the partnership or S Corporation didn't matter because there was no profit available to "spend" on these deductions.

Later, when the company started to make a profit, I terminated the S Corporation status by sending a letter to the IRS, and reverted back to C Corporation status because I needed more tax deductions to offset the income. I switched back to a C Corporation to take advantage of the medical and dental reimbursement plan and the retirement savings plan. The C Corporation also allows me to benefit from income splitting, that is, leaving some income in the corporation, which enjoys lower marginal income tax rates resulting in lower taxes.

Some people achieve this same effect by starting out as an LLC in the early years when there are business losses, and then "kill" the LLC when the business starts to make money. They immediately replace the LLC with a C Corporation to benefit from the tax breaks available to a C Corporation. This strategy can be a lot of trouble, especially if the business grows to any size at all. Reorganizing an existing business is a lot of work.

So What's The Bottom Line?

Well, after considering all the advantages and disadvantages of the different types of business organizations, I lean toward the corporation. The corporation's flexibility in tax planning and tax reduction makes it the winner for most people.

A Comparison of Business Organizations

	Proprietorship	Partnership	Corporation (S or C)	LLC
Best Suited For:	• Single owner business where taxes or product liability are not a concern	• Business with partners where taxes or product liability are not a concern	• Single or multiple owner business where owner(s) need(s) company funded fringe benefits and liability protection	• Single or multiple owner business where owner(s) need(s) limited liability but want to be taxed as a partnership • Real estate investment companies • Existing partnerships
Type of Entity:	• Inseparable from owner	• Inseparable from owner but can have debt or property in its name	• Separate legal entity	• Separate legal entity
Main Advantages:	• Inexpensive to set up • Few administrative duties	• Inexpensive to set up • Few administrative duties	• Limited liability, • Company paid fringe benefits (C corp.) • Tax savings through income splitting (C corp.) • Capital is easy to raise through sale of stock	• Limited liability, • Pass–through entity • Unlimited number of owners • Capital is easy to raise through sale of interests
Main Disadvantages:	• Unlimited liability • No tax benefits • Business dissolves upon death of owner	• Unlimited liability, also liable for partners' acts • No tax benefits • Legally dissolves upon change or death of partner	• Can be costly to form • More administrative duties • S corp. limited to 35 shareholders	• Can be costly to form • More administrative duties • Taxed like a partnership
Taxes:	• Owner is responsible • File Schedule C with Form 1040	• Partners are responsible • File Form 1065	• C corp. pays its own • S corp. passes through to owners • File Form 1120 • S corps. file 1120S	• Usually taxed as a partnership, but can be taxed as a corp. in some states • Usually Form 1065

Forming A Corporation

Most people think incorporating a business is a difficult and complex thing to do. Actually it's very simple. Basically all you need to do is file a document called "The Articles of Incorporation" with a state agency and pay a fee. The articles of incorporation is a simple document that satisfies the requirements of state law. It is filed with the secretary of state and provides information about the corporation that you want to form. It contains little more than your name and address, and the corporate name you want to use.

A little background...

Until the early 1900's, incorporating wasn't so easy. When the first corporations were formed, a business owner had to petition the state legislature to pass a special law allowing the business to operate as a corporation. Of course, having your own law passed is a complicated and expensive process - an option only available to those with enough money, influence, and legal experts to get the job done.

With the industrial boom of the early 1800's, the corporation became the preferred type of business organization. Operating as a corporation made it easier to obtain the enormous funds needed to build factories and railroads. Instead of going to the bank for a loan, entrepreneurs simply sold shares, or small pieces of their business, to anyone wanting to "share" in the huge potential profits of the venture. Legislatures soon found they were spending too much time granting corporate charters, and began to pass general corporation laws that made it much easier to incorporate a business.

In 1811, New York passed the first general corporation statute and began to enjoy tremendous revenues from corporations. Hungry for a piece of the revenue pie, the neighboring states of New Jersey and Delaware passed more liberal (easier to satisfy) corporate statutes by 1899. The Delaware law basically made incorporating a matter of filing a form with the secretary of state. Of course this lured many corporations away from New York and began the interstate competition for corporations that continues today.

Delaware remained the epicenter for corporations until 1969 when the American Bar Association developed a uniform set of corporation law based on the popular Delaware corporation statute. By simply adopting this "turn-key" set of laws called "The Model Business Corporation Act" any state could have its own set of modern corporation law by simply making The Model Act a part of its own law. Most states did just this. Today, the Model Act is the basis for corporate law in most states and single-handedly destroyed the primary advantage of incorporating in Delaware, which brings up an important question.

In Which State Should You Incorporate?

New York was the first to discover that making it easy for businesses to incorporate brings in generous revenues in the way of fees and taxes. New York was the first "best state to incorporate in" followed by New Jersey and then Delaware. Today the king of corporations is the State of Nevada. Why? Well the two most important reasons are that Nevada has no corporate income tax, and secondly, the shareholders of the corporation can remain anonymous.

So what state should you incorporate in? It's my opinion that you should incorporate in the state where you are doing business. That is, where your office is located. There are only two reasons to incorporate in another state, first, if you are going to have offices in many states, and second, for tax planning. If you are going to have offices in more than one state, Nevada makes a good choice because it is "friendly" to corporations. Also, since Nevada has no state corporate income tax, you can lower your taxes by shifting income there from a taxable state. Needless to say, this is a sophisticated tax strategy meant for those with large tax bills and a good CPA.

The bottom line...
It's best to incorporate in the state where you are located when you first start out. If you get offices in other states later, you can relocate your corporate headquarters then. Besides, if you incorporate in another state, you'll have to register the corporation in your state as a "foreign" or out-of-state corporation doing business in your own state.

THE INCORPORATING PROCESS

The incorporating process is very simple and consists of four basic steps; choosing a corporate name, filing your articles with the state, attending to some organizational matters like issuing stock, and setting up your corporate records book. Please read all of the steps and understand them fully before completing any step. A mistake could result in having to redo and refile paperwork, costing you time and money. As I said in the introduction, the process outlined here is applicable to any state. The last chapter will give attention to any state specific variations of this procedure.

Step 1. Choose your corporate name.
Step 2. File your paperwork with the state.
Step 3. Take care of organizational matters.
Step 4. Prepare a corporate record book.

Step 1. Choose a Corporate Name

The first step in organizing your corporation is selecting a name. Your corporate name must meet specific requirements outlined by State law. They are:

Requirement 1...
The name must show that you are a corporation. It must contain either "incorporated" "corporation" "company" or an abbreviation of one of these words like "inc." "corp." or "co.."

These words or their abbreviations tell the world that you are operating as a corporation. This way, other businesses, creditors, etc. know that you are not responsible for corporate obligations, and that any lawsuits must be brought against the corporation.

Requirement 2...
The corporate name must be different from corporate names being used in the state or any other name on file with the Secretary of State. This includes LLCs, out of state corporations doing business in the state, and registered trademarks. Also, your corporate name may not be "deceptively similar" to other names in use. This keeps companies from benefiting from the goodwill created by another company.

If another corporation has taken the name you want to use, all you'll need to do is add another word to the corporate name to meet this requirement. For example, if your last name is Brown and you want to use "Brown, Inc." as your corporate name, you'll probably find that another entrepreneur named Brown beat you to it. However, you can still use Brown in your corporate name if you simply add another word or initial. For example, you could name it

Brown Ventures, Inc., Brown Publishing, Inc., or Dean Brown, Inc. Oh, by the way, changing the corporate identifier doesn't change the name. That is, changing from "Inc." to "Corp." doesn't help, "Brown, Inc." and "Brown Corp." is the same corporate name.

Please note that if the corporate name you want to use is available according to the records of the Secretary of State, there may still be an unincorporated business like a sole proprietorship or partnership using the name. According to law, the business that uses the name first in a geographic location has the rights to the name. To check for these types of businesses, you can look in the white pages of your telephone directory. If you plan to do business in other cities, you may want to check those telephone directories too. If you want to do business state wide, regionally, or nationally, you may consider having your name researched by professionals and registered as a trademark with the U.S. Patent and Trademark office. Registering a trademark will give you the right to use the name in all 50 states. For more information on trademarks, see the book entitled "Trademarks, How to Name Your Business & Product" in the catalog at the back of this book.

Requirement 3...

The corporate name may not contain a word or phrase indicating that the company is organized to transact business for which it has not been approved. For example, your corporate name can't contain the word "insurance" unless the company has satisfied state requirements for incorporating as an insurance company. The same applies for other types of regulated businesses like banks, securities brokers, hospitals, physicians, etc.

Also, the corporate name may not imply that the corporation is affiliated with, or sponsored by, any fraternal, veteran's, service, religious, charitable, or professional organization unless the authorization is officially granted to the business and the authorization is certified in writing. For example, if you're not associated with the YMCA, you can't make "YMCA" a part of your corporate name. In addition, stay away from names that make your corporation sound like it's a part of the State or Federal government. Although using the word federal in your name is usually okay, be careful not to imply any governmental authority or affiliation.

Other considerations for choosing a name...

Assumed names, fictitious names and DBAs - An assumed name, sometimes called a fictitious name, is a feature of some state laws that allows a business to operate under more than one name. This can be quite convenient to the small business person who operates different businesses but does not want to have several corporations. Using an assumed name, most people initially name the corporation with their last name, something like Jones, Inc. They might then name their different companies to be more descriptive of separate product lines, like Quantum Computers, Inc., and Standard Computer Software Corporation. All of these would simply be different names, or aliases for the same corporation, that has only one set of books, and the same shareholders. To let the world know that the corporation, Jones Inc., and these other companies are the same, a notice to this effect is filed with a state or local official. We'll discuss this further in the last chapter.

Checking the availability of a corporate name...

Since you can't use a corporate name already taken by another corporation, documents submitted with such a name used by another corporation will be rejected. So, before filing your articles of incorporation, you'll want to check to see if another corporation is already using the name. In most states you can find out if "your" corporate name is available by simply calling the Secretary of State and checking.

Before you call, be sure of the name you wish to use, and that it contains one of the required "Inc." words. You should also have one or two additional names chosen in case your first choice is being used by another company. Checking the availability of your name should only take a couple of minutes. This is a good time to ask any questions you may have and double check the filing fees, etc.

The Secretary of State has computer access to all corporate names being used in the state. The role playing outlined below is designed for a telephone call, but of course face to face conversation will be the same. The conversation will basically go like this:

S/S: *Secretary of State's Office, may I help you?*

You: *Yes. I'd like to check the availability of a corporate name please. (The person will either check the name, or transfer you to the person who will.)*

S/S: *Okay. What is the name you'd like to check?*

You: *Brown Publishing, Inc.*
(The person will now check their computer for the name.)

S/S: *That name appears to be available. (That's great.)*

The Secretary of State will usually only say something like the "name appears to be available." That's because someone may walk into their office five minutes later and file paperwork using "your" name. There are no guarantees as to the availability of a name until your articles of incorporation are accepted.

If your first choice for a corporate name is already being used, the conversation will continue like this:

> *S/S:* *Brown Advertising does not appear to be available at this time. Are there any other names you'd like to check? (This is when your second and third choices come in handy.)*

> *You:* *Yes. What about Brown Communications, Inc.?*

> *S/S:* *(The person will now check for the new name.) That name does appear to be available at this time. (You've hit pay dirt.)*

If name checks by phone are not offered in your state, you'll have to go ahead and file your articles and hope for the best. If the name you like is already being used, the state will either fax, call, or write you with this information.

Step 2. File Your Paperwork

The paperwork you must file to incorporate a business is a document called the Articles Of Incorporation. Some states require that you file another document or two with your articles, but we'll cover that in the last chapter.

The Articles are easy to complete if you know basic information like your name, the corporation's name, and your address. The document usually provides information about five items, the corporation, the corporation's stock, the corporation's registered agent, the directors, and finally the incorporators of the corporation. The document on the next page is a typical articles of incorporation.

Completing the articles of incorporation is pretty simple. Be sure to type the form so that it can be accurately recorded by the Secretary of State. Most states require that the articles be typed. If you want to type the articles on your computer instead of using a typewriter, the forms in this book are available on a computer disk for IBM PC (Windows) or Mac compatible computers. For more information, please see the catalog at the back of the book. Now, let's go through the articles of incorporation one article at a time.

Article 1. Name…
This one is pretty simple. Just put your corporate name here. Make sure the name meets state requirements and includes a corporate identifier like "Inc." or Incorporated.

Article 2. Office…
Another easy one. Include here the street address of the corporation's principle office. Your home address is okay to use.

Example

ARTICLES OF INCORPORATION

Pursuant to Article 3.02 of the Texas Business Corporation Act, the undersigned incorporator submits these articles of Incorporation for the purpose of forming a for-profit corporation.

Article 1. The name of the Corporation is:

Consumer Publishing Corporation

Article 2. The principal office of the corporation is located at:

1234 Main Street, Houston, TX 12345

Article 3. The corporation's period of duration is perpetual.

Article 4. The corporation is authorized to issue one class of stock, that stock being 100,000 shares of no par value, common stock, with identical rights and privileges, the transfer of which is restricted according to the bylaws of the corporation.

Article 5. The purpose or purposes for which the corporation is organized is to engage in any lawful act or activity allowed by The Texas Business Corporation Act.

Article 6. The name of the corporation's registered agent, and the street address of the corporation's registered office is:

Dean Brown 1234 Main Street, Houston, TX 12345

Article 7. The name and street address of the sole incorporator of this corporation is:

Dean Brown 1234 Main Street, Houston, TX 12345

Optional Items:

Article 8. No Director shall be held liable to the corporation or its shareholders for monetary damages due to a breach of fiduciary duty, unless the breach is a result of self-dealing, intentional misconduct, or illegal actions.

In witness whereof, the undersigned incorporator has executed these Articles of Incorporation on the date below. The undersigned incorporator hereby declares, under penalty of perjury, that the statements made in the forgoing Articles of Incorporation are true, and that the incorporator is at least eighteen years of age.

Date: June 1, 1998

Signature of Incorporator: *Dean Brown*

Article 3. Duration...

The duration of the corporation is simply how long it will exist. If you are using the corporation to pursue a single project, you may wish to limit its life-span to the length of the project. Most businesses don't have a particular life-span. Most corporations will exist until they go out of business or the sole owner dies. In this case, the life of the corporation is said to be perpetual, or never ending. Unless you have a particular reason for doing otherwise, the period of duration for your corporation should be perpetual.

Article 4. Stock...

Let's talk about stock for a minute. Stock is issued to a corporation's share-holders (owners) to show that they own a part of the enterprise. In this article, you'll describe the stock your corporation will issue, the total number of shares, its par value, and any particular rights and privileges it has. Providing this information in the articles of incorporation makes it public information, available to all shareholders and potential shareholders.

Authorized Shares - The first piece of information we'll provide about the stock is the number of authorized shares. This is the total number of shares your corporation will ever have. You can only change this number with the approval of a majority of shareholders and by amending the articles of incorporation. Needless to say, authorizing too many shares is better than not authorizing enough. I usually authorize one hundred thousand or a million shares of stock unless I'm forming a corporation in a state where the filing fee for the articles of incorporation is based on the number of authorized shares. In such a case, I'll authorize the maximum number of shares I can without increasing the filing fee. Nevada, for example, will let you authorize 25,000 shares without incurring a higher filing fee than the $125 minimum. Issuing more than 25,000 shares your filing fee will increase.

Common vs. Preferred shares - There are basically two different types of stock your corporation can issue, common and preferred. Common stock is what corporations usually issue to shareholders. It's what they trade on the New York Stock Exchange. The holders of common stock choose the directors of the corporation by voting their shares at an annual shareholders meeting. They also get to vote on other important matters that affect the corporation. Common stock holders of larger corporations get paid a quarterly dividend based on corporate profits. If there are no profits, a dividend is not usually paid.

Preferred stock, on the other hand is more like a bond or promissory note. It carries a fixed dividend percentage rate. Holders of preferred stock get paid dividends first. If there are profits left after paying the preferred dividends, then dividends are paid to the common shareholders. That's why it's called preferred stock, dividends on it are paid first. There is a drawback however. As a trade-off for getting dividends first, preferred shareholders don't get to vote on matters affecting the corporation. Preferred stock is nonvoting. I occasionally talk to a reader who wants to issue preferred stock. My advice is not to. Issue common stock only.

Voting and Nonvoting Stock - Before we go on, let me point out that there are also two types of common stock - voting and nonvoting. Voting stock, of course gets to vote on matters that affect the corporation, nonvoting does not. Nonvoting stock comes in handy when you want to give someone ownership in the company but you don't want them to have the power to elect directors. Nonvoting stock comes in handy for issuing to your kids, investors, or anyone who wants ownership without voting power. To show the difference between voting and nonvoting, you will divide the stock into classes. If you want voting and nonvoting stock in your corporation, you should describe it in your articles of incorporation like this:

"The corporation is authorized to issue 100,000 shares of stock described as follows:

50,000 shares of voting common stock without par value designated as Class A.

50,000 shares of nonvoting common stock without par value designated as Class B."

Par Value - Par value of stock is a bookkeeping term that basically equates to price. That is, the par value of a share of stock is usually the price per share that a shareholder must pay to the corporation when buying the stock. It's really an outdated term because most stock issued these days is "no par" stock. That is, it has no fixed price per share. It is sold to different shareholders at different prices depending on the needs of the corporation.

Article 5. Purpose...
Some states require a purpose clause. A purpose clause simply states what the corporation's principal business is going to be. Once upon a time, you had to specifically state what type of business you were going to operate, but most states now accept the "general purpose clause" shown here. Using this clause, you can operate any type of business that you choose. This clause will also allow you to change the type of business your corporation transacts as you need.

Article 6. Registered agent...
A corporation's registered agent is the person appointed to accept legal documents on behalf of the corporation. If someone sues you, the papers will be served on the registered agent at the "registered office." Therefore, a registered agent, sometimes called a resident agent, must have a street address. You can be your own registered agent, and even use your home address. If you

choose to incorporate in a state where you do not have an office, you will need the services of a registered agent service company. Consumer Publishing can serve as a registered agent in Tennessee or Nevada.

Article 7. Incorporator...

The incorporator is simply the person who files the articles of incorporation with the state. The incorporator really has no rights except appointing the initial corporate directors. After the directors are appointed, the incorporator resigns.

Optional items...

There are many different things that are not required to be in your articles of incorporation that you can include, providing they are not prohibited by state law. Something I always include is a statement limiting the liability of the directors. As you can tell from reading it, it keeps lawsuit happy shareholders from suing you (the director) for money.

Delayed effective date - If you are incorporating toward the end of the year, you may want to include a delayed effective date of incorporation. For example, if you're incorporating in the month of December, and you aren't going to start your business until the first of the year, you can include a statement in your articles that says the filing won't be effective until January first. This way, you won't have to file any tax returns for this "short" tax year beginning in December. State and Federal agencies won't be expecting you to be open for business until after the first of January. To make sure the Secretary of State sees this, put a yellow Post-it® Note on the articles that says: "Notice: Delayed Effective Date."

All those involved in the corporation do not need to sign the Articles because they will be formally adopted by all shareholders and directors after the they are filed with the Secretary of State. So, only the person completing the Articles (the incorporator) needs to sign.

Now you are ready to file your Articles. You can either mail, send them by overnight courier, or take them to the Secretary of State's office yourself.

Step 3. Take Care of Organizational Matters

After your articles of incorporation are filed, State law requires that you take care of a few other important details before the organization of your corporation is complete. You must officially adopt the articles of incorporation and bylaws, elect officers, approve the corporate seal and issue stock. These actions are usually taken at a meeting known as the organizational meeting.

At the organizational meeting, all proposed directors, officers, and shareholders meet to discuss these organizational matters, take action on them and record the results as "minutes" of the meeting.

To make this easier than it sounds, a prewritten minutes of directors meeting has been included at the end of this chapter for your use. The form is called "Minutes of the Organizational Meeting of the Board of Directors." To use this form, all you'll need to do is read it carefully and insert the information pertaining to your corporation in the appropriate blanks. The next few pages will discuss topics and terminology related to completing the form.

Directors...

Although it is a legal "person" with rights of its own, a corporation can't walk, talk, think, or act for itself. It can't hold a pen to sign contracts. It can't go to the bank to make a deposit. It can't market its products or perform any of the physical tasks required to operate a business. Since it has no mental or physical capabilities, the business affairs of the corporation are managed and "directed" by directors. The group that oversees a corporation's activities is known as "the board of directors." Directors are like the guardians of an incompetent adult, who has rights, but can't think or act for him/herself. Directors meet from time to time to plan and approve actions the corporation will take to conduct its business.

Following correct procedure, directors are like trustees, charged by law to oversee the business affairs of the corporation. More like special consultants who come in periodically to plan and approve corporate actions, directors are usually not employees of the corporation. In return for their efforts, directors usually receive a token compensation, and other perks.

Deviating from the procedure envisioned by state law, the directors of large corporations don't actually oversee the business affairs of the corporation. In these corporations, directors are usually well known business people, celebrities, or former politicians who lend credibility to the corporation. In this case, being a director is more a position of status and the "directors" merely meet from time to time to "rubber stamp" what the officers they appointed have decided is best for the corporation. This rubber stamp approval of corporate action is not the correct procedure, but is reality in many cases.

Officers...

Although directors are responsible for managing and directing the business affairs of the corporation, they mostly oversee the "big picture." To manage the day to day activities of the corporation, the directors appoint and hire officers. Officers handle all of the daily decisions required to run a business, and the scope of their duties usually depends on the size of the corporation.

That is, the president of a corporation like Sears probably delegates the

ORGANIZATION OF A TYPICAL CORPORATION

SHAREHOLDERS ELECT AND CONTROL THE DIRECTORS THROUGH VOTING.

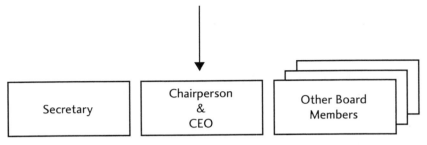

Secretary	Chairperson & CEO	Other Board Members

DIRECTORS OVERSEE THE BUSINESS AFFAIRS OF THE CORPORATION.
THEY DELEGATE DAY–TO–DAY MATTERS TO THE OFFICERS
WHICH THEY APPOINT AND HIRE.

Vice President	President / CEO	Secretary	Treasurer

OFFICERS RUN THE CORPORATION SUBJECT TO DIRECTOR CONTROL.

THE CORPORATION

important duty of selecting new store sites to a subordinate, merely checking in periodically to make sure things are running smoothly. In contrast, the presidential duties of a small business corporation would probably include everything from selecting the store location, to selling the merchandise. A corporation usually has the following officers. You can change the titles and responsibilities to meet your needs. You can also add officers and titles if you wish, having more than one vice-president for example.

President ....Carries out the most important functions.
Vice-President .Acts for the President when needed.
Secretary ....Responsible for corporate records and meetings.
Treasurer ....Manages the financial affairs of the corporation.

When managing the daily activities of the corporation, the president is generally responsible for the more important or glamorous responsibilities like signing contracts or developing strategies for the corporation. The vice-president fills in for the president when necessary, or assists the president. The secretary maintains corporate records and correlates the organizational affairs of the corporation. The treasurer is responsible for the financial welfare of the corporation, from obtaining loans, to overseeing the accounting department. Although large corporations can delegate duties the way state laws intended, the officer positions of a small corporation are usually filled by a single person who will carry out most, or all of these responsibilities.

Many times, in a small corporation, the directors and the officers are actually the same people who simply "wear different hats." That is, when you're carrying out director responsibilities, you're a director, and when taking care of officer duties, you're an officer. Officers are most always employees of the corporation. Being an employee of your own corporation is important because it makes you eligible for lucrative employee benefits, like retirement plans and hospitalization insurance. The corporation of course pays for these benefits.

Shareholders...

Now you know what roles the directors and officers play, but the most important players in the average corporation aren't the directors or the officers. The most important people are those for whom the corporation was formed - the stockholders. The stockholders are the people who started, and own the corporation for their mutual benefit. The stockholders invest money, property, or something else of value into the corporation. In return, the stockholders will own a part of the corporation relative to the amount they invested. These people provide the means by which the corporation is able to begin operating.

To provide evidence of their ownership and investment, the corporation will issue these individuals a stock certificate. That's why these people are called "stockholders." These stocks represent ownership in a particular corporation, and are similar to those bought and sold on the stock exchanges in New York. In fact, stocks of small corporations sometimes trade just as fervently as those on Wall Street. Of course, only the stocks of larger corporations are traded on an exchange.

Since we couldn't have a corporation without them, the stockholders are at the top of the power structure. They control the corporation for their common good by appointing the directors who will oversee the activities of the corporation. Ideally, in large corporations where shareholders are spread over a large geographic area, the directors are like independent observers appointed by the shareholders to help insure their interests are protected.

Of course, what's been described here is the textbook example of how a large corporation works, and is very different from how a small one works. However, all of this needed to be explained so that you might gain a complete understanding of all the participants in the corporate world. You may understand the process better by reviewing the diagram on page 36. Your corporation will look and function exactly like this diagram. Shareholders will start the corporation by giving money or property in exchange for its stock. The shareholders will then appoint directors to monitor their investment. Finally, since being a director isn't a full time calling, the directors appoint and hire officers to actually run the corporation on a daily basis.

Your corporation, however, will have one very important difference, only one or two people will hold most or all of these positions. Most small corporations will only have one or two people acting as all the directors, officers and stockholders. That's fine. I would suggest, however, that you fill at least two of the officer positions-those of president and secretary. A president is needed to run the day-to-day operations of the corporation like hiring, firing, dealing with the accountant, signing contracts, etc. The secretary is needed to keep up with the internal corporate paperwork-meeting minutes, issuing stock certificates, and drafting corporate resolutions.

When completing the minutes of organizational meeting form, put a nominal figure in the salary column if you haven't decided what the officer salaries will be. One hundred dollars per year will be okay. When you decide what the salaries will be, hold a director's meeting on the subject and make the change. The directors will officially approve of the salary, and this approval will be noted in the minutes of the meeting.

In reality, most people simply pay themselves whatever they can. Then, at the end of the year (at tax time), part of the total amount paid is allocated to officer salary and the rest to "regular" salary. The allocation is usually based on the amount of time spent performing officer duties relative to the time spent at other tasks. For example, if you paid yourself $50,000 and spent 10% of your time performing officer duties, then it would be reasonable to pay yourself a $5,000 officer salary and a $45,000 salary for your other efforts. (.10 X $50,000 = $5,000 and $50,000 - $5,000 = $45,000) You may want to speak with your accountant about this. I think most people just leave this blank until they know what they'll be able to pay themselves.

Issue the stock of the corporation...

A business corporation cannot exist without stockholders. Stockholders, or shareholders as they are often called, invest money in a corporation in exchange for a part or "share" of the corporation. In return for their investment, shareholders receive dividends based on the future earnings of the corporation or some other monetary reward. In many cases, shareholders invest in a corporation hoping that its value will increase and enable them to later sell their stock at a profit. Shareholders who buy stock in a corporation for its profit potential are known as investors. Shareholders like you who are not investors usually work for the corporation and receive a salary in addition to or instead of dividends.

There are basically two ways to buy stock in a corporation - either directly from the corporation, or in the open market. Initially, all stocks are purchased directly from the corporation that issued them. However, many shares are bought by investors who will sell them at some point in the future. This is how shares become available in the open market, investors selling them to other investors. There is such a demand for these shares as investments, huge exchanges like the New York Stock Exchange were created to facilitate the purchase and sell of these secondhand securities.

Unlike the investor who buys for speculation, you are buying stock in your corporation to start a company. Like most small business owners, you'll probably hold on to your stock and someday leave it to your kids. But, like the investor, you will still have to "purchase" the stock from your corporation and give something of value for it. You must bargain with the board of directors to determine a price acceptable to both you and the board. Your situation is a little different because you will play both the role of the prospective shareholder wanting to buy stock and the director wanting to receive something of acceptable value for it. In reality, however, prospective shareholders like yourself will give what they can afford for the stock and of course "the board" will accept your offer. In this case, issuing stock boils down to three things:

1. *Who will the shareholders be?*
2. *What percentage or part of the corporation will each person own?*
3. *How much will the shareholders pay for each share of stock?*

Once you know the answers to these questions, issuing the stock is simply a matter of completing the last section of the form entitled "Minutes of the Organizational Meeting of the Board of Directors" and issuing stock certificates to each new shareholder. Be sure to read the remainder of this section before issuing the stock. Also, remember the price per share of all initially issued shares must be the same.

Registration...

If you are starting a business and wish to attract investors by incorporating, are trying to make money from the sale of the stock, or will be paying commissions to a broker for the sale of the stock, you will need to register your stock with the State Securities Commission.

If you offer your stock to someone living outside the state, your stock issue will fall under Federal securities laws as an interstate offering. If you plan to make such an out-of-state offer, you may want to seek professional advice. If you don't want to "seek professional advice" make sure that the person to whom you are offering stock is in your state at the time of the "offer." This makes the offering an intrastate offering, regulated by State securities law.

The registration of securities, stocks, bonds, partnership interests, etc., is a process designed to protect investors from fraudulent securities offerings. It involves the gathering of information related to the offering, and the drafting of a document called a prospectus. A prospectus is an informational booklet designed to give investors enough information about the company and the offering to make an informed buying decision. Under the securities laws of most states, some stock offerings are exempt from registration while others are not. If you are simply incorporating your existing business or issuing stock to family members or other organizers and officers of the corporation that live in your state, state law provides for you an exemption from registration. Generally, the issuance of stock is exempt from registration if:

1. *The stock is only issued to corporate officers and organizers, people who actively participate in the operation and management of the corporation.*

2. *The stock is issued by the corporation and not a securities dealer.*

3. *The issue is not advertised or offered to the general public. (Outsiders)*

4. *There are fewer than 10 shareholders when all the stock is issued. (Husband and wife count as one shareholder.)*

The main point to remember is this. Registration is designed to protect consumers from fraudulent stock offerings. So, do NOT offer stock to someone unless they are intimately familiar with you and the financial condition of the corporation.

Authorized vs. issued shares...

If you conclude your stock is exempt from registration, you may proceed with its issue. But before you issue stock, let's discuss the difference between authorized shares of stock and issued shares of stock. "Authorized shares" is the number of shares set by the Articles of Incorporation that the board of directors is "authorized" to issue. The board of directors is the body that controls the issuance of stock. In large corporations, this authorized limit on the total number of shares prevents the board from issuing too many shares. Too many new shares lower the value of your stock.

The board may issue all the shares now, or issue some now, and some later. Your Articles of Incorporation state the number of shares that the corporation is authorized to issue and make this number a matter of public record for all to see. The number of authorized shares equals the total number of shares that may be issued now, or at some point in the future. Issued shares is the number of shares "issued" or distributed to shareholders. Only issued shares count for ownership purposes. Shares that are not issued are called authorized but unissued shares. They are technically worthless until they are issued to a shareholder. Usually when a corporation issues shares of stock to its initial shareholders, a few shares are left unissued so that they may be issued later to new investors, family members etc.

It is a good idea not to issue (distribute) all of the authorized shares now, because you may need a few shares to issue later. You may want to issue some stock to a son or daughter entering the business, or to a new business partner. The main point to remember is that only issued shares count for ownership. Take the following example for a corporation that has 1,000 authorized (another word for total available) shares of stock, and two owners:

Owner A is issued 100 shares   100/200=50% ownership
(Number owned divided by total issued.)

Owner B is issued 100 shares   100/200=50% ownership
(Number owned divided by total issued.)

The two shareholders in this example own 50% of the corporation because the 800 unissued shares are not considered in the calculation. One thousand authorized shares less 200 issued shares leaves 800 available for future use. Since only the 200 issued shares count for ownership, owners with 100 shares each own one half of the corporation. (One hundred is half of two hundred.) Only issued shares count for ownership percentages.

Multiple shareholders…

Issuing stock in a corporation with more than one owner can sometimes be tricky, especially if the percentage of ownership or consideration is unequal. Let's take a minute here to talk about the different combinations and possible solutions. (Consideration is the money or property given for stock.)

For the purposes of these examples, let's say that there are three owners (shareholders) in the corporation and 100,000 authorized shares of stock. Remember from the previous section, it's a good idea not to issue all of your authorized shares so we won't in these examples. Many readers that I talk with get caught up in the stock's price per share upon issue. Don't worry about the price per share. It doesn't matter. Instead, concentrate on how much of the corporation each shareholder will own. The price per share will simply be a function of how much of the corporation the shareholder owns and the amount given for the stock.

Equal ownership / Equal consideration - This is an easy one. All three shareholders put in an equal amount of cash (the amount doesn't matter) and will divide ownership evenly, one third each. To make the math easy, let's issue each owner 10,000 shares of stock, leaving 70,000 shares unissued. A total of 30,000 shares (10,000 + 10,000 + 10,000) of stock will be issued. Let's check our math, 30,000 total issued shares, divided by 10,000 shares issued to each owner equals .333 or 1/3 ownership each. Each shareholder will invest an equal amount of money, based on how much money the corporation needs to start operations. To show their ownership, we'll issue one stock certificate to each shareholder for 10,000 shares.

Equal ownership / Unequal consideration - This is a typical example. People of different financial means often start businesses together. Some owners put in money, and some put in effort. This situation occurs when a certain amount of money is needed to start the business, and only one person can contribute it.

For this example, let's say that $10,000 is needed to start the business. The best way to handle this is to have all three shareholders contribute the same amount of money for their stock, and the additional amount is given as a loan. Two of the shareholders will put in what they can, say $500 each. The third shareholder puts in $500 too. Now the business has $1,500 of the $10,000 it needs. The additional $8,500 needed will be loaned to the corporation by the third shareholder. The officers of the corporation will sign a promissory note guaranteeing payment of the $9,500 to the third shareholder.

Again, let's issue each owner 10,000 shares of stock, leaving 70,000 shares unissued. A total of 30,000 shares (10,000 + 10,000 + 10,000) of stock will be issued. Let's check our math, 30,000 total issued divided by 10,000 shares to each owner equals .333 or 1/3 ownership each. To show their ownership, we'll issue one stock certificate to each shareholder for 10,000 shares.

Unequal ownership / Unequal consideration - This is similar to the first example. In this example there are three shareholders. Shareholder 1 will own 10 percent of the corporation, shareholder 2 will own 20 percent and shareholder 3 will own the remaining 70 percent. All we do here is simply issue the needed number of shares to each person, and adjust the consideration to match. For example, lets issue 10,000 of our 100,000 shares to make the numbers easy to work with. We will give the first shareholder 1,000 shares, the second shareholder 2,000 shares, and the third shareholder 7,000 shares for a total of 10,000 shares issued. (1,000 is 10% of 10,000 and 2,000 is 20% of 10,000 and 7,000 is 70% of 10,000) For consideration, the shareholders contribute $1,000, $2,000 and $7,000 respectively. If the shareholders don't have that much money, they could contribute $100, $200, and $700 respectively. Still too much? Then let them contribute $10, $20, and $70 respectively. The amount of the consideration doesn't matter as long as it makes the ownership percentages what we need them to be.

Consideration...

Stock in a corporation represents various rights and privileges to the shareholder. So, in exchange for the stock of a corporation something of value must be given. The payment given to a corporation for its stock is known as consideration. State law governs the type of consideration you give for your stock. You can pay money, give property, or have already provided labor or services to the corporation for which you were not paid.

Some states have a minimum capital requirement, that is, a minimum amount of money is required to be in the company's bank account before operations can begin. If there is no minimum capital requirement in your state, any amount of consideration approved by the Board of Directors is acceptable. This amount can be all cash, all property, all services, or various combinations of the three. Since giving consideration other than money can cause tax problems, you should see your CPA before doing so. However, I wouldn't see my CPA if I were simply putting a computer and some office furniture into the corporation. A CPA should be consulted if you are going to put vehicles, real estate, expensive equipment, or other big dollar items into the corporation.

Please note that money given to the corporation doesn't "disappear." In reality, the corporation will spend this much money just opening its doors and you would have put money into the corporation anyway. The corporation will spend this amount reimbursing you for filing fees, taxes, buying office supplies, printing stationery, paying rent and so forth. If your initial cash contribution isn't enough to get the corporation up and running, you'll have to put more money into the corporation from time to time. If you do, you can account for this contribution in three ways:

1. *You can put money into the corporation in return for additional stock. This is usually done when other business associates are involved. (Partners)*

2. *You can put money into the corporation, issue no more stock and simply call this an owner's contribution. This is usually done when there is only one shareholder. This money is not taxed when taken out of the corporation.*

3. *You can put money into the corporation, call it a loan, and receive the money back with interest. Discuss this with your CPA first. This is the preferred method. The best way to do it is to set up an account on your books called something like "Payable to Shareholder" and whenever you lend money to the company, account for it with this account.*

If you give property for the stock, you'll need to transfer the title of the property to the corporation, and provide a bill of sale. If there is not enough room to record the payment on the director's minutes, use an additional sheet of paper, and file it with your corporate records. This is a corporate matter that doesn't involve the State. Sometimes, giving property or services for your corporation's stock leads to tax problems, and you should see your CPA accordingly. Fortunately, this is not usually the case. If you simply give property to your new corporation in exchange for at least 80% of the stock, you usually don't have to worry about taxes. Internal Revenue Code Section 351 calls this a tax-free exchange and allows it. However, exchanging property in the following cases will lead to problems. If you want to exchange property for stock in a manner similar to any of these examples, or are transferring property to the corporation to avoid taxes, see your CPA or tax advisor first. A list of property transfers to avoid:

1. *An exchange of property to a corporation when you will own less than eighty percent of the stock.*

2. *An exchange where you receive cash, or property, or benefits other than stock for your property.*

3. *An exchange where your liabilities against the property exceed your adjusted basis in that property.*

4. *An exchange of property that has increased in value since you bought it.*

Many people retain ownership to the property and simply rent, or lease it to the corporation. This way you can receive lease payments from the corporation for its use, making it lease or rental income to you. This is a good way to get money out of the company without paying Social Security taxes. (Rental income is only subject to regular income taxes.) One word of caution here, be careful leasing vehicles or dangerous equipment to the company. If someone gets injured by the vehicle or equipment, the injured party may try to recover from you as the lessor of the equipment.

Issuing stock certificates...

Although stock certificates are not money and this is only an analogy, you may compare stock certificates to checks in a checkbook and authorized shares to the amount of money in your checking account. Stock certificates and checks are similar, but of course are not the same. Instead of representing money like checks do, stock certificates represent shares of ownership in a corporation. When you write a check, you give someone money. When you issue certificates, you give someone ownership in your corporation. With a checkbook, you can write checks in any dollar amount to as many people as you want until you either run out of money or out of checks. With stock, you can issue certificates for any number of shares to as many people as you want until you either run out of authorized shares or out of certificates.

Please note that you are not limited to using the certificates included with this book. You can use as many stock certificates as you like. Only a few certificates are included in this book because most corporations are one or two person corporations and therefore only need one or two certificates. If you need more stock certificates, blue or green certificates like the ones in this book, or color stock certificates in a customized corporate outfit are available from Consumer Publishing. The certificates in the corporate outfit have your company's name typeset on them.

To issue stock certificates to each shareholder, you must complete the face of the certificate by typing the name of the corporation, the name of the shareholder, the date, the state of incorporation, the number of authorized shares, the par value, and the number of shares being issued to the shareholder all in their appropriate spaces. Next, number the certificates sequentially, (01, 02, 03, 04, 05...) and have the President and Secretary of the corporation sign the certificates at the bottom left and right. The circle near the bottom is where you will press the corporation's seal. See the example certificate at the end of the chapter.

On the back, do not complete the section that begins with "For value received." This section is completed when, and if you ever sell your stock. Completing this section is like endorsing a check, and makes the certificate transferable.

Corporation bylaws...

The bylaws of the corporation are the rules by which it operates. Just as a city has laws for its citizens, a corporation has laws for its shareholders, directors, and officers. A standard set of corporate bylaws for your use is at the end of the chapter. The only thing you'll need to do with the bylaws is read them, and become familiar with your corporate rules. Become especially familiar with the procedure a shareholder must follow before selling any stock as outlined in article four.

Also, note in article five you must complete the time and date of the annual meeting of the corporation. This can be any date and time that is convenient for you that allows enough time to prepare financial reports for the year just ended. It is important that you hold an annual meeting or at least sign the prewritten minutes because the directors and officers are only appointed for one year terms and are reappointed every year at this time. Remember, the minutes of the annual shareholders meeting have already been prepared, so all you really need to do is sign and date them. Most people never really have an annual shareholder's meeting, they just sign the minutes and file them away.

Since these bylaws are standard and written for most corporations, you may feel the need to customize or add to the bylaws. You may want to customize your bylaws in these areas:

- *Dividends - if, when, and how much will be paid.*

- *Officer salaries.*

- *Directors compensation - if, when, and how much will be paid.*

- *Further conditions for the transfer of stock, like what to do in the event of the death of a shareholder. Will the stock be left to the spouse, or must it be sold back to the corporation?*

- *What happens if the corporation dissolves? How will the assets be distributed?*

- *At some point in the future a shareholder may want to leave the corporation and sell his stock. How do you determine what the stock is worth? It's better to determine this in advance to prevent arguments. Many corporations value stock by taking the stockholder's equity (Assets - Liabilities) and dividing it by the number of shares. Other corporations have director meetings about once every six months to set a value for the shares. The method is up to you.*

Step 4. Prepare a Corporate Record Book

Since you are required by law to keep meticulous records of the activities of your corporation, you will need to set up and maintain a corporate record book. Properly organized records are one of the first things the IRS will ask to see if you ever get audited. Plus, if you intend to seek financing for your new venture, your banker will want to see your corporate records as well. The corporate record book is the only proof that your corporation is properly organized and maintained so don't skip this step.

Although you can organize them in any convenient manner, most people use a corporate records book, or corporate "kit" as they are sometimes called, for storing their records. A record book is simply a nice binder with divided sections for storing your company documents, minutes, and certificates and includes the corporate seal. When preparing a corporate record book, you have two choices, either prepare your own, or purchase one.

If you choose to purchase one and are unable to find corporate supplies in your area, corporate kits and corporate seals are available from Consumer Publishing. Please see the order form in the back of the book for more information. Corporate kits are shipped within 24 hours. Next day service is also available. Corporate kits are available for C and S Corporations as well as nonprofit corporations, professional corporations, and close corporations.

Each outfit includes:

- *A deluxe binder with the corporate name gold embossed on the spine,*
- *A matching slip case to protect your records from dust,*
- *A corporate seal,*
- *20 Stock certificates imprinted with the corporate name,*
- *A stock transfer ledger,*
- *Preprinted minutes and bylaws,*
- *A special forms section and a review of IRS requirements for S corporations,*
- *Medical and dental reimbursement plans described in Chapter One,*
- *Annual meeting forms.*

If you prefer to prepare your own corporate kit, you'll need to visit a legal stationary or lawyer supply store and purchase the following:

- *A three ring binder,*
- *At least 8 tabbed index dividers to divide the book into sections,*
- *Pre-punched three ring binder paper to keep minutes on,*
- *A corporate seal.*

A corporate seal should be included with the corporate record book because the seal is how the corporation "signs" contracts, minutes, and other official documents like stock certificates. The seal is maintained by the corporate secretary and is used to show that the corporation approves of documents that the seal is applied to. After you have all of your supplies together, you should assemble them as follows.

1. *Prepare these headings for the tabbed index dividers; APPLICATIONS & PERMITS; STATE FILINGS; BYLAWS; MINUTES; STOCK CERTIFICATES; S-ELECTION; FORMS; and JOURNAL LEDGER.*

2. *Three hole punch the documents already filed with the state and/or the IRS, as well as the directors meeting minutes completed in the previous step and insert them into the appropriate sections of the corporate record book.*

3. *Copy or remove the bylaws from this chapter and insert them into the BYLAWS section.*

4. *Copy or remove the prewritten minute forms from this chapter and insert them into the MINUTES section. Remember to make copies of the blank originals for your future minute keeping needs. The minutes from all your meetings will be kept in this section.*

5. *Prepare a separate list of stockholders, directors, and officers of the corporation and include these lists in the JOURNAL LEDGER section. These lists may seem insignificant but are required by law. Be sure to update these lists if anything changes.*

Record keeping...
Every list of pros and cons of incorporating I've ever seen usually lists increased record keeping at the top of the cons list. Although there is more record keeping involved with a corporation, listing increased record keeping as the top reason not to incorporate is shortsighted. Corporate record keeping is not a big deal.

To understand the reason a corporation requires more records than an unincorporated business, lets review for a minute. Remember that a corporation is a separate and distinct entity with legal rights of its own that acts for or on the behalf of its shareholders. Owners incorporate their business to allow them to act through the corporation. Although the corporation is a legal "person" it cannot act for itself. So, to allow the corporation to carry out its business, the shareholders appoint directors to manage and direct the business affairs of the corporation. The directors act like the trustees of an incompetent adult, planning and directing the activities of the corporation. Since the directors are acting in a trustee type arrangement, states require that everything done by the directors on behalf on the corporation be documented. That's why every time a meeting is held to take action on behalf of the corporation, it must be documented, and minutes of the meeting must be recorded.

Another reason extensive records of corporate activities are kept is the shareholder. Remember that when corporate laws were originally drafted, the idea of a one or two person corporation had not been considered. Laws were originally drafted to match the textbook example of a corporation with many investor shareholders. In such a case, the shareholders, officers, and directors were all different people. Laws were written to protect the shareholder from unscrupulous directors and officers who would run a corporation broke to make themselves rich. This is another reason things must be documented and annual shareholders meetings held, to keep officers and directors honest by documenting their every move.

Of course, your corporation will probably be formed with less that four shareholders. These shareholders will probably be the officers, and directors as well. In this case, the shareholders will know the events within their corporation. Considering this, record keeping may seem like a waste but you must remember one thing. Operating as a corporation can give you great benefits, legally, and in the area of taxes too. To make sure that these abilities are not abused, states and the IRS require that you keep records of all corporate activities. Basically records must be kept of all important events within the corporation.

Here is a list of the records you must keep for your corporation. These records must be available for shareholder inspection and accordingly should be kept at the offices of the corporation in an orderly manner.

- *Minutes of all shareholder and director meetings, generally for the last 3 years.*
- *Appropriate accounting records and financial reports.*
- *An alphabetical list of all shareholders with their addresses.*
- *An alphabetical list of all directors with their business addresses.*
- *An alphabetical list of all officers with their business addresses.*
- *Copies of all formal documents used to incorporate the business.*
- *All written communications to shareholders for the past 3 years.*
- *Financial statements for the past 3 years.*
- *A copy of the most recent annual report.*
- *All contracts entered into by the corporation.*
- *Amendments to, or changes in the corporate bylaws.*
- *Records of stock issues and transfers.*
- *Promissory notes.*
- *Life insurance policies held on corporate officers and directors.*

Holding meetings...

The recording of meetings and even the meeting itself need not be made overly formalized. For example, many people formally call the meeting to order; formally ask for turns to speak; formally make, and second motions; and formally adjourn the meeting. This formality comes from directors meetings of large corporations, and is not necessary for small corporate meetings.

When holding a meeting, all you need to do is sit down, discuss what needs to be done, vote on the matter, summarize it on paper, and have everyone sign it. The best way to do this is to write down everything that happens on a plain piece of paper, summarize and organize the information, then transfer it to a formal minutes type form.

If you have no other meetings, you must have an annual shareholders meeting to "discuss" the results of operations for the year with the shareholders. Many people don't actually hold a meeting, they just sign the minutes of the meeting and file it in your corporate records binder. Before using them, make extra copies of the forms in this chapter for your future use.

This concludes the incorporating process. Now, let's talk about a few things you'll need to do after you've incorporated your business.

If you're incorporating an existing business, read on. There's a section for some things you'll need to consider.

Other Considerations

In this last part of this chapter, we'll cover a couple of things that may not concern everyone, the S Corporation election, and incorporating an existing business.

S Corporation election...

This section will cover the subject of S corporations, what they are, and how to form one. Before we proceed, let me make one thing perfectly clear. An S Corporation is not a special kind of corporation. It is simply a corporation that elects special tax treatment allowed under Subchapter S of the Internal Revenue Tax Code. Being an S Corporation is a tax matter only.

When you complete the formation of your corporation by following the steps outlined in this book, a new taxpaying entity will exist. The Internal Revenue Service and your state department of revenue will expect to receive taxes on the income of your new corporation and the income of its employees. It's almost as if you had a newborn baby and the baby was expected to start paying taxes immediately.

Just as individuals may choose to file as either "Single" "Married" "Head of household" etc., corporations have similar filing options. A corporation may choose to file as either a "C" corporation, or an "S" corporation. If a corporation chooses to be a C Corporation, it will be taxed according to Subchapter C of the IRS tax code. If a corporation chooses to be an S Corporation, it will be taxed according to Subchapter S of the IRS tax code.

All new corporations are classified by the IRS as C corporations. You don't have to do anything to be a C Corporation. But, if you think that filing as an S Corporation will lower your taxes, you must elect to be treated as an S Corporation and then notify the IRS of your choice. Notifying the IRS is a simple procedure that is accomplished by filing a single form with them, Form 2553.

To be treated as an S Corporation, you may also have to file a form with your state. To see if you do, contact the state department of revenue. Please remember that time limits exist regarding the filing of S Corporation forms. Filing a form late may exclude you from electing S Corporation status.

Prior to filing the Form 2553 with the IRS and perhaps a similar form with your state department of revenue, you'll need to get director and shareholder approval to make the S Corporation election. Director approval can be granted in a meeting of the directors. Their approval will be noted in the minutes of the meeting. Do not send this form to the IRS. This form is for your records only. Keep it in your corporate records book.

Shareholder approval is also recorded on Form 2553. All you need to do is simply record the information for each shareholder and have them sign and date the form. Be sure to keep a copy of this form in your corporate record book. Send the original with original signatures to the IRS via certified mail. Technically, election of S Corporation status is subject to IRS approval. Accordingly, you will receive notification by mail.

If you live in a community property state or own the shares of stock jointly with another person, then both people will be listed as shareholders and both will sign the form. Each person will show that they own half the number of shares jointly owned. For example, if a husband owns stock in a corporation and lives in a community property state, his wife legally owns half of the stock. So, both names, SSN's, and signatures will appear on the form. The number of shares that he owns will be divided in half for the purpose of completing the form. Half the number of shares will appear next to his name and half will appear next to hers.

Which is best, an S Corporation or a C Corporation? It depends on your personal tax situation but here's my opinion. Newer corporations that have net losses should be S Corporation and more mature corporations that are making profits should be C corporations. Many people start out as an

S Corporation and then change filing status when the company starts to make a profit.

Completing the form…
Completing the IRS form 2553 is not difficult. The only hard part is remembering to file it before you run out of time. The form must be filed before the 16th day of the third month of the tax year to be effective for your first year in business. If you miss this deadline, your S Corporation election won't be effective until next year. Does that mean that a corporation formed June 1st is out of luck? Well, the instructions would make you to think so, but it's not the case. You see, the tax year of a corporation formed June 1st doesn't begin until June 1. This makes August 15th the deadline for filing. My advice-file the form when you get incorporated and send it via Certified Mail. Most importantly, don't complete the back of the form. The back is for special situations and trust entities.

When you're finished, send the form to the same IRS office where you mail your personal tax return-listed in the instructions to the form. If you have any questions, call the IRS at 1-800-829-1040.

Form **2553**

(Rev. September 1997)

Department of the Treasury
Internal Revenue Service

Election by a Small Business Corporation

(Under section 1362 of the Internal Revenue Code)

▶ **For Paperwork Reduction Act Notice, see page 2 of instructions.**

▶ **See separate instructions.**

OMB No. 1545-0146

Notes:

1. *This election to be an S corporation can be accepted only if all the tests are met under* **Who May Elect** *on page 1 of the instructions; all signatures in Parts I and III are originals (no photocopies); and the exact name and address of the corporation and other required form information are provided.*

2. *Do not file* **Form 1120S,** *U.S. Income Tax Return for an S Corporation, for any tax year before the year the election takes effect.*

3. *If the corporation was in existence before the effective date of this election, see* **Taxes an S Corporation May Owe** *on page 1 of the instructions.*

Part I — Election Information

Please Type or Print

Name of corporation (see instructions)	**A** Employer identification number
Number, street, and room or suite no. (If a P.O. box, see instructions.)	**B** Date incorporated
City or town, state, and ZIP code	**C** State of incorporation

D Election is to be effective for tax year beginning (month, day, year) . . . . ▶ / /

E Name and title of officer or legal representative who the IRS may call for more information

F Telephone number of officer or legal representative ( )

G If the corporation changed its name or address after applying for the EIN shown in **A** above, check this box . . . . ▶ ☐

H If this election takes effect for the first tax year the corporation exists, enter month, day, and year of the **earliest** of the following: (1) date the corporation first had shareholders, (2) date the corporation first had assets, or (3) date the corporation began doing business . . . . ▶ / /

I Selected tax year: Annual return will be filed for tax year ending (month and day) ▶ ----------------------------------

If the tax year ends on any date other than December 31, except for an automatic 52-53-week tax year ending with reference to the month of December, you **must** complete Part II on the back. If the date you enter is the ending date of an automatic 52-53-week tax year, write "52-53-week year" to the right of the date. See Temporary Regulations section 1.441-2T(e)(3).

J Name and address of each shareholder; shareholder's spouse having a community property interest in the corporation's stock; and each tenant in common, joint tenant, and tenant by the entirety. (A husband and wife (and their estates) are counted as one shareholder in determining the number of shareholders without regard to the manner in which the stock is owned.)	K Shareholders' Consent Statement. Under penalties of perjury, we declare that we consent to the election of the above-named corporation to be an S corporation under section 1362(a) and that we have examined this consent statement, including accompanying schedules and statements, and to the best of our knowledge and belief, it is true, correct, and complete. We understand our consent is binding and may not be withdrawn after the corporation has made a valid election. (Shareholders sign and date below.)		**L** Stock owned		**M** Social security number or employer identification number (see instructions)	**N** Share-holder's tax year ends (month and day)
	Signature	Date	Number of shares	Dates acquired		

Under penalties of perjury, I declare that I have examined this election, including accompanying schedules and statements, and to the best of my knowledge and belief, it is true, correct, and complete.

Signature of officer ▶   Title ▶   Date ▶

See Parts II and III on back.   Cat. No. 18629R   Form **2553** (Rev. 9-97)

Part II   Selection of Fiscal Tax Year (All corporations using this part must complete item O and item P, Q, or R.)

O Check the applicable box to indicate whether the corporation is:

1. ☐ A new corporation adopting the tax year entered in item I, Part I.

2. ☐ An existing corporation retaining the tax year entered in item I, Part I.

3. ☐ An existing corporation changing to the tax year entered in item I, Part I.

P Complete item P if the corporation is using the expeditious approval provisions of Rev. Proc. 87-32, 1987-2 C.B. 396, to request **(1)** a natural business year (as defined in section 4.01(1) of Rev. Proc. 87-32) or **(2)** a year that satisfies the ownership tax year test in section 4.01(2) of Rev. Proc. 87-32. Check the applicable box below to indicate the representation statement the corporation is making as required under section 4 of Rev. Proc. 87-32.

1. Natural Business Year ▶ ☐ I represent that the corporation is retaining or changing to a tax year that coincides with its natural business year as defined in section 4.01(1) of Rev. Proc. 87-32 and as verified by its satisfaction of the requirements of section 4.02(1) of Rev. Proc. 87-32. In addition, if the corporation is changing to a natural business year as defined in section 4.01(1), I further represent that such tax year results in less deferral of income to the owners than the corporation's present tax year. I also represent that the corporation is not described in section 3.01(2) of Rev. Proc. 87-32. (See instructions for additional information that must be attached.)

2. Ownership Tax Year ▶ ☐ I represent that shareholders holding more than half of the shares of the stock (as of the first day of the tax year to which the request relates) of the corporation have the same tax year or are concurrently changing to the tax year that the corporation adopts, retains, or changes to per item I, Part I. I also represent that the corporation is not described in section 3.01(2) of Rev. Proc. 87-32.

Note: *If you do not use item P and the corporation wants a fiscal tax year, complete either item Q or R below. Item Q is used to request a fiscal tax year based on a business purpose and to make a back-up section 444 election. Item R is used to make a regular section 444 election.*

Q Business Purpose—To request a fiscal tax year based on a business purpose, you must check box Q1 and pay a user fee. See instructions for details. You may also check box Q2 and/or box Q3.

1. Check here ▶ ☐ if the fiscal year entered in item I, Part I, is requested under the provisions of section 6.03 of Rev. Proc. 87-32. Attach to Form 2553 a statement showing the business purpose for the requested fiscal year. See instructions for additional information that must be attached.

2. Check here ▶ ☐ to show that the corporation intends to make a back-up section 444 election in the event the corporation's business purpose request is not approved by the IRS. (See instructions for more information.)

3. Check here ▶ ☐ to show that the corporation agrees to adopt or change to a tax year ending December 31 if necessary for the IRS to accept this election for S corporation status in the event (1) the corporation's business purpose request is not approved and the corporation makes a back-up section 444 election, but is ultimately not qualified to make a section 444 election, or (2) the corporation's business purpose request is not approved and the corporation did not make a back-up section 444 election.

R Section 444 Election—To make a section 444 election, you must check box R1 and you may also check box R2.

1. Check here ▶ ☐ to show the corporation will make, if qualified, a section 444 election to have the fiscal tax year shown in item I, Part I. To make the election, you must complete **Form 8716**, Election To Have a Tax Year Other Than a Required Tax Year, and either attach it to Form 2553 or file it separately.

2. Check here ▶ ☐ to show that the corporation agrees to adopt or change to a tax year ending December 31 if necessary for the IRS to accept this election for S corporation status in the event the corporation is ultimately not qualified to make a section 444 election.

Part III   Qualified Subchapter S Trust (QSST) Election Under Section 1361(d)(2)*

Income beneficiary's name and address	Social security number
Trust's name and address	Employer identification number

Date on which stock of the corporation was transferred to the trust (month, day, year) . . . . ▶ ____ / ____ / ____

In order for the trust named above to be a QSST and thus a qualifying shareholder of the S corporation for which this Form 2553 is filed, I hereby make the election under section 1361(d)(2). Under penalties of perjury, I certify that the trust meets the definitional requirements of section 1361(d)(3) and that all other information provided in Part III is true, correct, and complete.

_____   _____
Signature of income beneficiary or signature and title of legal representative or other qualified person making the election   Date

*Use Part III to make the QSST election only if stock of the corporation has been transferred to the trust on or before the date on which the corporation makes its election to be an S corporation. The QSST election must be made and filed separately if stock of the corporation is transferred to the trust after the date on which the corporation makes the S election.

 Printed on recycled paper   *U.S. Government Printing Office: 1997 - 432-190/60239

Instructions for Form 2553

(Revised September 1997)

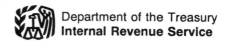

Department of the Treasury
Internal Revenue Service

Election by a Small Business Corporation

Section references are to the Internal Revenue Code unless otherwise noted.

General Instructions

Purpose.— To elect to be an S corporation, a corporation must file Form 2553. The election permits the income of the S corporation to be taxed to the shareholders of the corporation rather than to the corporation itself, except as noted below under **Taxes an S Corporation May Owe.**

Who May Elect.— A corporation may elect to be an S corporation only if it meets all of the following tests:

1. It is a domestic corporation.

2. It has no more than 75 shareholders. A husband and wife (and their estates) are treated as one shareholder for this requirement. All other persons are treated as separate shareholders.

3. Its only shareholders are individuals, estates, certain trusts described in section 1361(c)(2)(A), or, for tax years beginning after 1997, exempt organizations described in section 401(a) or 501(c)(3). Trustees of trusts that want to make the election under section 1361(e)(3) to be an electing small business trust should see Notice 97-12, 1997-3 I.R.B. 11.

Note: *See the instructions for Part III regarding qualified subchapter S trusts.*

4. It has no nonresident alien shareholders.

5. It has only one class of stock (disregarding differences in voting rights). Generally, a corporation is treated as having only one class of stock if all outstanding shares of the corporation's stock confer identical rights to distribution and liquidation proceeds. See Regulations section 1.1361-1(l) for more details.

6. It is not one of the following ineligible corporations:

a. A bank or thrift institution that uses the reserve method of accounting for bad debts under section 585;

b. An insurance company subject to tax under the rules of subchapter L of the Code;

c. A corporation that has elected to be treated as a possessions corporation under section 936; or

d. A domestic international sales corporation (DISC) or former DISC.

7. It has a permitted tax year as required by section 1378 or makes a section 444 election to have a tax year other than a permitted tax year. Section 1378 defines a permitted tax year as a tax year ending December 31, or any other tax year for which the corporation establishes a business purpose to the satisfaction of the IRS. See Part II for details on requesting a fiscal tax year based on a business purpose or on making a section 444 election.

8. Each shareholder consents as explained in the instructions for column K.

See sections 1361, 1362, and 1378 for additional information on the above tests.

An election can be made by a parent S corporation to treat the assets, liabilities, and items of income, deduction, and credit of an eligible wholly-owned subsidiary as those of the parent. For details, see Notice 97-4, 1997-2 I.R.B. 24.

Taxes an S Corporation May Owe.— An S corporation may owe income tax in the following instances:

1. If, at the end of any tax year, the corporation had accumulated earnings and profits, and its passive investment income under section 1362(d)(3) is more than 25% of its gross receipts, the corporation may owe tax on its excess net passive income.

2. A corporation with net recognized built-in gain (as defined in section 1374(d)(2)) may owe tax on its built-in gains.

3. A corporation that claimed investment credit before its first year as an S corporation will be liable for any investment credit recapture tax.

4. A corporation that used the LIFO inventory method for the year immediately preceding its first year as an S corporation may owe an additional tax due to LIFO recapture.

For more details on these taxes, see the Instructions for Form 1120S.

Where To File.— File this election with the Internal Revenue Service Center listed below.

If the corporation's principal business, office, or agency is located in	Use the following Internal Revenue Service Center address
New Jersey, New York (New York City and counties of Nassau, Rockland, Suffolk, and Westchester)	Holtsville, NY 00501
New York (all other counties), Connecticut, Maine, Massachusetts, New Hampshire, Rhode Island, Vermont	Andover, MA 05501
Florida, Georgia, South Carolina	Atlanta, GA 39901
Indiana, Kentucky, Michigan, Ohio, West Virginia	Cincinnati, OH 45999
Kansas, New Mexico, Oklahoma, Texas	Austin, TX 73301
Alaska, Arizona, California (counties of Alpine, Amador, Butte, Calaveras, Colusa, Contra Costa, Del Norte, El Dorado, Glenn, Humboldt, Lake, Lassen, Marin, Mendocino, Modoc, Napa, Nevada, Placer, Plumas, Sacramento, San Joaquin, Shasta, Sierra, Siskiyou, Solano, Sonoma, Sutter, Tehama, Trinity, Yolo, and Yuba), Colorado, Idaho, Montana, Nebraska, Nevada, North Dakota, Oregon, South Dakota, Utah, Washington, Wyoming	Ogden, UT 84201
California (all other counties), Hawaii	Fresno, CA 93888
Illinois, Iowa, Minnesota, Missouri, Wisconsin	Kansas City, MO 64999
Alabama, Arkansas, Louisiana, Mississippi, North Carolina, Tennessee	Memphis, TN 37501
Delaware, District of Columbia, Maryland, Pennsylvania, Virginia	Philadelphia, PA 19255

When To Make the Election.— Complete and file Form 2553 **(a)** at any time before the 16th day of the 3rd month of the tax year, if filed during the tax year the election is to take effect, or **(b)** at any time during the preceding tax year. An election made no later than 2 months and 15 days after the beginning of a tax year that is less than 2½ months long is treated as timely made for that tax year. An election made after the 15th day of the 3rd month but before the end of the tax year is effective for the next year. For example, if a calendar tax year

corporation makes the election in April 1998, it is effective for the corporation's 1999 calendar tax year.

However, an election made after the due date will be accepted as timely filed if the corporation can show that the failure to file on time was due to reasonable cause. To request relief for a late election, the corporation generally must request a private letter ruling and pay a user fee in accordance with Rev. Proc. 97-1, 1997-1 I.R.B. 11 (or its successor). But if the election is filed within 6 months of its due date and the original due date for filing the corporation's initial Form 1120S has not passed, the ruling and user fee requirements do not apply. To request relief in this case, write "FILED PURSUANT TO REV. PROC. 97-40" at the top of page 1 of Form 2553, attach a statement explaining the reason for failing to file the election on time, and file Form 2553 as otherwise instructed. See Rev. Proc. 97-40, 1997-33 I.R.B. 50, for more details.

See Regulations section 1.1362-6(b)(3)(iii) for how to obtain relief for an inadvertent invalid election if the corporation filed a timely election, but one or more shareholders did not file a timely consent.

Acceptance or Nonacceptance of Election.— The service center will notify the corporation if its election is accepted and when it will take effect. The corporation will also be notified if its election is not accepted. The corporation should generally receive a determination on its election within 60 days after it has filed Form 2553. If box Q1 in Part II is checked on page 2, the corporation will receive a ruling letter from the IRS in Washington, DC, that either approves or denies the selected tax year. When box Q1 is checked, it will generally take an additional 90 days for the Form 2553 to be accepted.

Do not file Form 1120S for any tax year before the year the election takes effect. If the corporation is now required to file **Form 1120**, U.S. Corporation Income Tax Return, or any other applicable tax return, continue filing it until the election takes effect.

Care should be exercised to ensure that the IRS receives the election. If the corporation is not notified of acceptance or nonacceptance of its election within 3 months of date of filing (date mailed), or within 6 months if box Q1 is checked, take follow-up action by corresponding with the service center where the corporation filed the election. If the IRS questions whether Form 2553 was filed, an acceptable proof of filing is **(a)** certified or registered mail receipt (timely filed) from the U.S. Postal Service or its equivalent from a designated private delivery service (see Notice 97-26, 1997-17 I.R.B. 6); **(b)** Form 2553 with accepted stamp; **(c)** Form 2553 with stamped IRS received date; or **(d)** IRS letter stating that Form 2553 has been accepted.

End of Election.— Once the election is made, it stays in effect until it is terminated. If the election is terminated in a tax year beginning after 1996, the corporation (or a successor corporation) can make another election on Form 2553 only with IRS consent for any tax year before the 5th tax year after the first tax year in which the termination took effect. See Regulations section 1.1362-5 for more details.

Cat. No. 49978N

Specific Instructions

Part I

Note: *All corporations must complete Part I.*

Name and Address of Corporation.— Enter the true corporate name as stated in the corporate charter or other legal document creating it. If the corporation's mailing address is the same as someone else's, such as a shareholder's, enter "c/o" and this person's name following the name of the corporation. Include the suite, room, or other unit number after the street address. If the Post Office does not deliver to the street address and the corporation has a P.O. box, show the box number instead of the street address. If the corporation changed its name or address after applying for its employer identification number, be sure to check the box in item G of Part I.

Item A. Employer Identification Number (EIN).— If the corporation has applied for an EIN but has not received it, enter "applied for." If the corporation does not have an EIN, it should apply for one on **Form SS-4,** Application for Employer Identification Number. You can order Form SS-4 by calling 1-800-TAX-FORM (1-800-829-3676).

Item D. Effective Date of Election.— Enter the beginning effective date (month, day, year) of the tax year requested for the S corporation. Generally, this will be the beginning effective date of the tax year for which the ending effective date is required to be shown in item I, Part I. For a new corporation (first year the corporation exists) it will generally be the date required to be shown in item H, Part I. The tax year of a new corporation starts on the date that it has shareholders, acquires assets, or begins doing business, whichever happens first. If the effective date for item D for a newly formed corporation is later than the date in item H, the corporation should file Form 1120 or Form 1120-A for the tax period between these dates.

Column K. Shareholders' Consent Statement.— Each shareholder who owns (or is deemed to own) stock at the time the election is made must consent to the election. If the election is made during the corporation's tax year for which it first takes effect, any person who held stock at any time during the part of that year that occurs before the election is made, must consent to the election, even though the person may have sold or transferred his or her stock before the election is made.

An election made during the first 2½ months of the tax year is effective for the following tax year if any person who held stock in the corporation during the part of the tax year before the election was made, and who did not hold stock at the time the election was made, did not consent to the election.

Each shareholder consents by signing and dating in column K or signing and dating a separate consent statement described below. The following special rules apply in determining who must sign the consent statement.

- If a husband and wife have a community interest in the stock or in the income from it, both must consent.

- Each tenant in common, joint tenant, and tenant by the entirety must consent.

- A minor's consent is made by the minor, legal representative of the minor, or a natural or adoptive parent of the minor if no legal representative has been appointed.

- The consent of an estate is made by the executor or administrator.

- The consent of an electing small business trust is made by the trustee.

- If the stock is owned by a trust (other than an electing small business trust), the deemed owner of the trust must consent. See section 1361(c)(2) for details regarding trusts that are permitted to be shareholders and rules for determining who is the deemed owner.

*Continuation sheet or separate consent statement.—*If you need a continuation sheet or use a separate consent statement, attach it to Form 2553. The separate consent statement must contain the name, address, and EIN of the corporation and the shareholder information requested in columns J through N of Part I. If you want, you may combine all the shareholders' consents in one statement.

Column L.— Enter the number of shares of stock each shareholder owns and the dates the stock was acquired. If the election is made during the corporation's tax year for which it first takes effect, do not list the shares of stock for those shareholders who sold or transferred all of their stock before the election was made. However, these shareholders must still consent to the election for it to be effective for the tax year.

Column M.— Enter the social security number of each shareholder who is an individual. Enter the EIN of each shareholder that is an estate, a qualified trust, or an exempt organization.

Column N.— Enter the month and day that each shareholder's tax year ends. If a shareholder is changing his or her tax year, enter the tax year the shareholder is changing to, and attach an explanation indicating the present tax year and the basis for the change (e.g., automatic revenue procedure or letter ruling request).

Signature.— Form 2553 must be signed by the president, treasurer, assistant treasurer, chief accounting officer, or other corporate officer (such as tax officer) authorized to sign.

Part II

Complete Part II if you selected a tax year ending on any date other than December 31 (other than a 52-53-week tax year ending with reference to the month of December).

Box P1.— Attach a statement showing separately for each month the amount of gross receipts for the most recent 47 months as required by section 4.03(3) of Rev. Proc. 87-32, 1987-2 C.B. 396. A corporation that does not have a 47-month period of gross receipts cannot establish a natural business year under section 4.01(1).

Box Q1.— For examples of an acceptable business purpose for requesting a fiscal tax year, see Rev. Rul. 87-57, 1987-2 C.B. 117.

In addition to a statement showing the business purpose for the requested fiscal year, you must attach the other information necessary to meet the ruling request requirements of Rev. Proc. 97-1 (or its successor). Also attach a statement that shows separately the amount of gross receipts from sales or services (and inventory costs, if applicable) for each of the 36 months preceding the effective date of the election to be an S corporation. If the corporation has been in existence for fewer than 36 months, submit figures for the period of existence.

If you check box Q1, you will be charged a $250 user fee (subject to change). Do not pay the fee when filing Form 2553. The service center will send Form 2553 to the IRS in Washington, DC, who, in turn, will notify the corporation that the fee is due.

Box Q2.— If the corporation makes a back-up section 444 election for which it is qualified, then the election will take effect in the event the business purpose request is not approved. In some cases, the tax year requested under the back-up section 444 election may be different than the tax year requested under business purpose. See **Form 8716,** Election To Have a Tax Year Other Than a Required Tax Year, for details on making a back-up section 444 election.

Boxes Q2 and R2.— If the corporation is not qualified to make the section 444 election after making the item Q2 back-up section 444 election or indicating its intention to make the election in item R1, and therefore it later files a calendar year return, it should write "Section 444 Election Not Made" in the top left corner of the first calendar year Form 1120S it files.

Part III

Certain qualified subchapter S trusts (QSSTs) may make the QSST election required by section 1361(d)(2) in Part III. Part III may be used to make the QSST election only if corporate stock has been transferred to the trust on or before the date on which the corporation makes its election to be an S corporation. However, a statement can be used instead of Part III to make the election.

Note: *Use Part III **only** if you make the election in Part I (i.e., Form 2553 cannot be filed with only Part III completed).*

The deemed owner of the QSST must also consent to the S corporation election in column K, page 1, of Form 2553. See section 1361 (c)(2).

Printed on recycled paper   *U.S. Government Printing Office: 1997 - 432-190/60241

MINUTES OF A SPECIAL MEETING OF THE BOARD OF DIRECTORS
OF

_____

Pursuant to the laws of the state in which this corporation is organized, and its bylaws, a meeting of the Directors of the above named Corporation was held at the offices of the corporation. The meeting was held on the _____ day of _____ at _____ o'clock PM/am. Present at the meeting was a quorum of directors, and all have signed their names below. As evidenced by their signatures, the directors hereby waive any meeting notice that may be required. The meeting was duly called to order and the following items of business were resolved.

1. It is decided that in the best interest of the stockholders the Corporation should elect federal taxation treatment under Subchapter S of the Internal Revenue Code as provided by the Internal Revenue Service, which would allow the Corporation to be taxed as a partnership, with the income or loss of the Corporation "passing through" to the stockholders. Consent and agreement of the stockholders will be evidenced by their signatures on Federal Tax Form Number 2553, a copy of which shall be included in the records of the Corporation. By electing tax treatment under Subchapter S, the Corporation will be required to use a calendar year with the tax year ending December 31, of each year.

2. All directors hereby approve of the action.

Having concluded all current business, the meeting was duly concluded.

Date:

Signature of Corporate Secretary _____

Chapter Two

Incorporating An Existing Business

Since an existing business has employees, leases, existing liabilities, bank accounts and other contractual arrangements, incorporating a preexisting business is not quite as simple as incorporating a new one. It's more complicated and will take more time. It's more than simply changing stationery.

Because a corporation is a separate and distinct entity and not simply an extension of the owner, incorporating an existing business is not as simple as just changing the name and doing business as usual. After incorporating, the corporation will actually be doing business with your customers, selling your products, making your loan payments and so on.

If you wish to conduct business as a corporation, the corporation will, in effect, need to "take your place" and formally adopt all contracts you've undertaken to conduct business. In some cases, the corporation may simply ratify the contracts that you have entered. In other cases, the old contracts will need to be voided and new ones entered into. In any case, the business that you have known and operated in the past will legally cease to exist, and the corporation will take its place as a totally new entity. It's almost as if you sold your business and its assets to the corporation.

Actually, if you transfer all your company's assets to the new corporation, you have, in effect, "sold" your business and its assets to the corporation. For this, the corporation will pay you with its stock. When this happens, the corporation basically owns your business, and you own the stock of the corporation. This is how you become separated from your business, thus gaining personal liability protection, and generous tax benefits.

Now that you understand the basics of incorporating a preexisting business, we need to discuss some of the details you'll need to consider when incorporating. However, at this point a word of caution is in order. Incorporating a preexisting business is a fairly straightforward event, but if you don't have a working knowledge of contracts and business law, you may be asking for trouble by going it alone.

Before beginning this process, you may want to do some research on contract law. Many books on the subject are available at your local bookstore or library. Also, your CPA is a good source of information. CPA's have formal training in business law and contracts, and your's may be able to help. As a last resort, you may want to consider hiring an experienced lawyer.

Please understand that this book was written to help you incorporate a business without a lawyer. Since incorporating an existing business includes areas of law beyond the scope of this book, some of which could take volumes to explain, an attempt to fully cover these areas will not be made. This is merely a basic outline of things you'll need to consider when incorporating an existing business, and is in no way to be considered a complete discourse on the subject, or a how to manual. Also, please remember that transferring property to a corporation may have tax implications, and you should see your CPA before doing anything.

When incorporating an existing business, you must first formally dissolve the old business. Any property held by the existing business will again be held by you personally. After you regain title to the property, there are basically two ways of proceeding:

1. *You can keep some of the property in your name personally, or*
2. *You can simply transfer everything to the corporation.*

If you choose to keep some of the business assets in your name, you may do so for the following reasons:

1. *To help maintain control when you are not the only shareholder, and*
2. *To receive personal income at a lower tax rate.*

In a corporation where you are not the only shareholder, it is important to retain as much control over the corporation as possible. One way of exercising control is through your voting stock. Another way is to control the assets that the corporation needs to operate. Simply stated, when the equipment needed to operate is under your control, you will usually be treated more fairly by other shareholders because you have the ability to "take your equipment and go home" when things don't go your way.

Secondly, keeping property out of the corporation can be very tax advantageous, especially if your salary income is high. When you retain title to property the corporation needs to operate, you can lease the property back to the corporation, and in return, receive lease payments. You can then lower the taxable effect of these lease payments with depreciation and other expenses related to the property's operation.

Usually, when a preexisting business is incorporated, everything, or most everything, is transferred to the corporation. This might include all the company assets, liabilities, and other contracts. Assets are usually transferred by conveying your title in them to the corporation. Liabilities, and other contracts are transferred to the corporation when the corporation formally adopts them.

Basically, you will "transfer and assign all your rights" in an item to the corporation with a written agreement stating that you do so. If the item has a title or deed, new documents must be prepared to show that the corporation now legally owns it.

The corporation must then formally adopt and approve everything that is done. To do this you will need to prepare director's consents to corporate action stating that the directors "approve and adopt" everything that is done. Also, if deeds or titles are involved, the corporation president will sign the documents needed to transfer the assets to the corporation. If you "transfer" all your business assets to your corporation, you should do so in return for the stock that the corporation will issue to you. This way, you will reduce or eliminate any chance that the transfers will cause tax problems. Assets to be transferred will include things like:

- *Cash in the bank*
- *Accounts receivable (Money your customers owe)*
- *Notes receivable (Other monies owed)*
- *Inventory*
- *Prepaid Expenses (Insurance)*
- *Deposits*
- *Cars and other vehicles*
- *Plant equipment & machinery*
- *Office equipment & computers*
- *Buildings*
- *Land*

Cash...

Transferring assets like cash is an easy thing to do. It's done by opening a new bank account in the name of the corporation, and putting the cash from your old account into the corporation's. You will actually close your old account and transfer all the funds with a check made payable to the corporation. You will then be authorized by corporate resolution to write checks on this new account. You will no longer "own" this money, because the corporation will.

However, by owning the stock of the corporation, you still indirectly "own" the money. But, you will no longer be able to dip into this cash whenever you please, because it now is the property of the corporation. But don't worry, the tax advantages gained by incorporating will make it worth the inconvenience.

Accounts receivable...

Accounts receivable is a formal contractual agreement between you and your customers in which they promise to pay you for goods and services provided to them. Since your business has actually ceased to exist, you'll need to assign your "rights" to collect this money to the corporation. All monies received in the future should be deposited into the corporate account, and you should notify your customers to make their checks payable to the corporation. This is a good chance to let your customers know that you have incorporated your business.

Notes receivable…

Notes receivable are like accounts receivable, except that notes receivable usually have promissory notes to back them up. For example, if you own a car lot where you sometimes finance your customer's purchases, your customers will sign a note promising to pay a fixed amount of money at certain intervals. When these promissory notes were made, they were made on behalf of your old business, which no longer exists. Therefore, you'll need to "assign the rights to collect payments" to the corporation, and similarly, tell the borrowers to make their payments to the corporation.

Miscellaneous assets…

Miscellaneous assets like inventory, prepaid expenses, office furniture, computers, and deposits are usually transferred to the corporation when the stock is issued. Documentation will include a listing in the corporate records that the property is being transferred to the corporation in exchange for corporate stock. For things like computers, and other small, yet expensive items, you will also need to give the corporation a "Bill of Sale" so that the corporation may prove it has legal title to the property. This is necessary to enable the corporation to sell the item in the future.

Assets with titles or deeds…

Some assets, like cars, machinery, buildings, and other larger items, have a title or a deed that shows who legally owns them. The titles and/or deeds to these items will need to be redone and re-filed in the name of the corporation. This may involve lawyers, title companies, and local governments, all of which will cost you time and money. However, for reasons listed above, these are sometimes not transferred to the corporation.

Liabilities…

For a minute, lets discuss the other side of the balance sheet, the liabilities side. Before incorporating, you are personally responsible for all your business's liabilities and loans. Since you now want your corporation to make these payments, the corporation will need to formally adopt the debts as its own. To do this, you will need to meet with your banker and other creditors to arrange for the notes and other liabilities to become the corporation's.

At best, the creditors will totally release you from the debts in exchange for new promissory notes signed by the corporation. This is best for you, because you will no longer be responsible for the payments, and your personal assets will probably not be taken to collect the debts.

In reality however, the creditors will not only want you to stay on the notes, but they will also insist that the corporation be made responsible as well. Of course, the corporation must become liable for the loans. Otherwise, the corporation will be making payments on your personal debt. Obviously, the corporation can't do this, because the IRS would consider these payments as taxable income to you.

Other contracts...

Since there are many contracts involved in operating a business, it will be easy to overlook some. Contracts entered into by you will not be enforceable by the corporation, and this could cause problems. Some contracts, like insurance policies, may be changed by transferring the policy to the corporation and having the corporation formally adopt it. Other contracts, like leases or employment agreements should be formally rewritten and entered into by the corporation. This will make enforcing these contracts easier for the corporation, while reducing some of your personal liability exposure. While the incorporation of an existing business includes many variables, I hope that this short discussion on the subject has been helpful to you.

Partnership agreements...

A partnership agreement is a special contract entered into by the partners of a business that is organized as a partnership. A partnership agreement is used to outline the basic "rules" by which the partnership will operate. All partners are bound by this agreement. The following list outlines some, but not all of the items covered in a typical partnership agreement:

- *Who "owns" the business and how much of the business each partner owns*
- *How income and expenses will be split between the partners*
- *What happens to business assets if the partnership splits up*
- *Who will manage the business*
- *Who takes care of the money*
- *Whether one partner can sign contracts without the other's approval*
- *Salaries and other compensation*
- *The length of time for which the partnership will exist*
- *The purpose of the partnership*

If you are currently operating your business as a partnership and want to incorporate, you'll need to do things a little differently. You see, corporations do not have "partnership" agreements. Instead, corporations have bylaws. Corporation bylaws should address most of the items listed above. After incorporating, your bylaws will determine how the business is operated. Accordingly, you should no longer use a partnership agreement if you incorporate. All of the items addressed in your current partnership agreement should be addressed by your corporation bylaws instead.

You're Done

This is the end of the chapter. On the next few pages, you'll find some of the forms needed to incorporate your business. The articles of incorporation for your use is found in the last chapter.

Oh, be sure to review chapter five. It outlines a few things you'll need to do before commencing operations - thinks like getting a Federal tax ID number, permits, etc. for your new business.

MINUTES OF THE ORGANIZATIONAL MEETING OF THE BOARD OF DIRECTORS
of

Pursuant to State Law, a meeting was held to complete the organization of the corporation. The meeting was held on the _____ day of _____ , at _____ o'clock _____ AM/PM. at the principal office of the corporation.

Present at the meeting were the incorporator, and the director(s), officer(s) and shareholder(s) named herein. As evidenced by their attendance and their signatures on the reverse, all directors, officers, and shareholders hereby waive any notice of the meeting that may be required by law. The incorporator duly called the meeting to order and the following items of business were resolved.

DIRECTORS
The incorporator, being all of the incorporators of the corporation, elected the person(s) named below to be director(s) of the corporation until the first annual shareholders meeting at which directors are elected or until new or replacement directors are elected. With the duties of the incorporator being completed, the incorporator resigned. A motion was duly made and seconded that the corporation adopt all pre-incorporation transactions entered into by the incorporator. The Chairperson of the Board presided over the remainder of the meeting.

_____   _____
Director - Chairperson   Director

_____   _____
Director   Director

OFFICERS
As their duties are outlined in the corporation bylaws, the Board unanimously elected the following individuals to be officers of the corporation—their respective titles below their name, and their annual salary to the right. These individuals will be officers until which time officers are either reelected or replaced. The president of the corporation was unanimously elected to serve as chairperson of the board of directors. Each person elected to an office accepted their appointment. The president noted that being an officer of the corporation did not preclude officers from holding other salaried positions within the corporation.

_____   _____
President / Chairperson of the Board of Directors   Pres. Salary

_____   _____
Vice-President   V.P. Salary

_____   _____
Secretary   Sec. Salary

_____   _____
Treasurer   Treas. Salary

ARTICLES OF INCORPORATION
A copy of the Articles of Incorporation filed with the State on _____ was presented at the meeting. The articles were approved by the directors of the corporation, and it was agreed that the corporate secretary shall place the articles in the corporate records book.

CORPORATE SEAL
The secretary presented at the meeting a proposed corporate seal. After a short discussion, a motion was made and duly seconded that the seal presented at the meeting be adopted as the seal of the corporation. The president noted that the seal shall remain in the custody of the corporate secretary along with the record book of the corporation.

The corporate secretary was directed to place an impression of the seal in the space to the right of this paragraph.

BYLAWS

A copy of the proposed bylaws for the corporation was presented at the meeting and was considered by the board. Upon motion duly made and seconded it was resolved that the bylaws presented at the meeting shall be the bylaws of the corporation. It was further agreed that the corporate secretary shall include a copy of the bylaws in the corporate records book.

BANK ACCOUNT

The authority by which a bank account may be opened for the corporation is granted by a separate resolution. The corporate secretary was asked to include a copy of that resolution with the corporate records book.

ACCOUNTING PERIOD

Upon motion duly made and seconded it is hereby resolved that the accounting period of the corporation shall end on _____ . It was noted by the president that the corporation must have a December 31 year end to elect IRS Subchapter S status.

ORGANIZATIONAL EXPENSES

After motion duly made and seconded, is was unanimously approved for the corporation to incur, pay, and reimburse any reasonable expenses related to the formation of the corporation. The president noted that organizational expenses of the corporation must be amortized over a period of 60 months.

STOCK

The stock of the corporation was issued under the direction of the Board of Directors. The members of the Board stated that they believe all State and Federal requirements relating to the issuance of the stock of the corporation have been met. Accordingly, a notice that the stock of the corporation is unregistered shall be placed on the certificates. The Board further stated that the stock shall be offered as Section 1244 stock and the issuance shall meet the requirements of IRS Section 1244. The president noted that by meeting the qualifications of IRS Section 1244, shareholders will receive preferential tax treatment in the event of a loss in the value of their stock. Verbal offers to purchase stock in the corporation were made by the individuals listed below and accepted by the Board of Directors. The individuals stated that the shares of stock were purchased for their own account and would not be traded publicly. The corporate secretary presented a stock certificate form at the meeting and it was approved by the board. The secretary will issue certificates to each shareholder and impress the corporate seal on the face of each certificate. Certificates will be signed by the President and Secretary of the Corporation.

Name	No. of Shares	% Ownership	Payment Given *
Name	No. of Shares	% Ownership	Payment Given *
Name	No. of Shares	% Ownership	Payment Given *
Name	No. of Shares	% Ownership	Payment Given *

* If needed, payment may be listed on a separate sheet of paper.

_____
Signature of Corporate Secretary

_____
Date

BYLAWS

of

The following shall be known as the Bylaws of the Corporation, the Bylaws being rules of self government of the Corporation. These bylaws are the set of rules by which the Corporation operates on a daily basis and settles disputes that may arise from time to time; and they are binding on all those associated with the Corporation either now, or in the future. If the Bylaws are found to be inconsistent with State Law, then State Law will override. The Bylaws may be amended by the Directors provided there is a majority of Directors votes favoring the amendments.

Article One

Purpose

The Corporation may take advantage of the rights granted to it by State law, and engage in any business allowed by State Business Corporation Law.

Article Two

Duration

The Corporation has perpetual duration and succession in its corporate name and will exist until such time that the Board of Directors elects to end its existence.

Article Three

Powers

The Corporation has the powers given by State Business Corporation Law, to do all things necessary or practical to carry out its business and affairs including without limitation, the power to sue, make contracts, deal in property of any kind, make investments, borrow or lend money, be a part of another entity, or conduct its business in any way allowed by the laws of this State.

Article Four

Stock

The shares of the Corporation will be common stock, with full voting rights and identical rights and privileges, with no par value. The issuance of shares will be governed by the Board of Directors, as will be the consideration to be paid for the shares, which will meet the requirements of State Business Corporation Law. The Corporation through its Board of Directors may issue fractional shares, acquire its own shares, declare and pay cash or stock dividends, or issue certificates.

In order to insure the continued existence of the Corporation, the transfer of shares of the Corporation to any individual or other entity will be restricted in the manner described herein. No shares may be transferred on the books of the Corporation unless the number of shares are first offered to the Corporation, and then to the other shareholders on a right of first refusal basis, the corporation having first option. This option to purchase the stock will expire in thirty (30) days from when offered. If the option is not exercised within the stated period, the Shareholder may dispose of the shares in any manner he wishes. The share certificates shall bear the following notice: RESTRICTED STOCK

Article Five
Meetings

Regular Meetings
The Corporation may hold any number of meetings to conduct its business. At a minimum, it will hold an annual Shareholders' meeting at which the Directors will review with the Shareholders the operating results of the Corporation for the prior year, hold elections for Directors, and conduct any other business that may be necessary at that time. Unless decided otherwise at the time, the place and time for the annual Shareholders' meeting will be at the offices of the Corporation on the day of at o'clock am/PM, each year. The Secretary will give proper notice to the Shareholders as may be required by law, however that notice may be waived by the Shareholder by submitting a signed waiver either before or after the meeting, or by his attendance at the meeting. Meetings may be held in or out of this State. Minutes must be taken by the Secretary for inclusion in the Corporate Records.

Special Meetings
The Corporation may hold meetings from time to time at such times and places that may be convenient. These meetings may be Directors meetings or Shareholder meetings or combined Director and Shareholder meetings. Special Shareholder meetings may be called by The Board of Directors or demanded in writing by the holders of ten percent or more shares. Special Director meetings may be called by the Chairman, the President, or any two Directors. The Corporate Secretary will give proper notice as may be required by law, however that notice may be waived by the individual by submitting a signed waiver either before or after the meeting, or by his attendance at the meeting. Meetings may be held in or out of this State. Minutes must be taken by the Secretary for inclusion in the Corporate Records.

Article Six
Voting

From time to time it may be necessary for a Director or Shareholder to vote on issues brought before a meeting. No voting may take place at a meeting unless there is a quorum present. That is, a quorum of Directors must be present at a meeting before any Director may vote, and likewise a quorum of Shareholders must be present at a meeting before any Shareholder may vote. A quorum of Directors at a meeting is defined as a majority of the number of Directors. A quorum of Shareholders at a meeting is defined as a majority of the shares entitled to vote. If a quorum is present at a meeting, action on a matter may be passed if the number of votes favoring the action is cast by a majority. For voting purposes, a Director may cast one vote, and a Shareholder may cast one vote for each share held except in the case of director elections when voting is cumulative. A Shareholder may vote in person or by proxy.

Article Seven
Action Without Meeting

Directors or Shareholders may approve actions without a formal meeting if all entitled to vote on a matter consent to taking such action without a meeting. A majority still is required to pass actions without a meeting. The action must be evidenced by a written consent describing the action taken, signed by the Directors or Shareholders (depending on which group is taking the action) indicating each signer's vote or abstention on the matter, and it must be delivered to the Corporate Secretary for inclusion with the Corporate Records.

Article Eight
Directors

All corporate powers will be exercised by, or under the authority of, and the business affairs of the Corporation managed under the direction of, its Board of Directors. The Board may consist of one or more individuals, who need not need be Shareholders or residents of this state. The terms of the initial Directors or subsequently elected Directors will end at the next Shareholders' meeting following their election, at which time new Directors will be elected or the current Directors will be reelected.

A director may resign at any time by delivering a written notice to the Corporation. A Director may be removed at any time with or without cause if the number of votes cast to remove him exceeds the number of votes cast not to remove him. Vacancies on the Board will be filled by the Shareholders in the manner described above.

The Directors of the Corporation are not liable to either the Corporation or its Shareholders for monetary damages for a breach of fiduciary duties unless the breach involves disloyalty to the Corporation or its Shareholders, acts or omissions not in good faith, or self dealing. The Corporation may indemnify the Directors or Officers who are named as defendants in litigation relating to Corporate affairs and the Directors or Officers role therein.

Article Nine
Officers

The officers of the Corporation will be initially appointed by the Board of Directors. The officers of the Corporation will be at least those required by State law, and any other officers that the Board of Directors may deem necessary. The duties and responsibilities of the Officers will be set by, and will be under the continued direction of, the Directors. Officers may be removed at any time with or without cause, and may resign at any time by delivering written notice to the Board of Directors. If allowed by state law, one person may hold more than one officer position.

President
The President is the principal executive officer of the Corporation and in general supervises and directs the daily business operations of the Corporation, subject to the direction of the Board of Directors. The President is also the proper official to execute contracts, share certificates, and any other document that may be required on behalf of the Corporation. The President shall also preside at all meetings of Directors or meetings of Shareholders.

Secretary
The Corporate Secretary will in general be responsible for the records of the Corporation which generally includes keeping minutes at any meeting, giving proper notice of any meeting, maintaining the Director and Shareholder registers and transfer records; and along with the President, sign stock certificates of the Corporation.

Vice President
The Corporate Vice-President if appointed will be responsible for duties to be assigned by the Board of Directors.

Treasurer
The Corporate treasurer if appointed will be responsible for duties to be assigned by the Board of Directors.

Other Officers
The directors may appoint other officers as they deem necessary.

CERTIFICATE NUMBER

01

NUMBER OF SHARES

5,000

Example **CERTIFICATE OF STOCK**

CONSUMER PUBLISHING CORP.

This Certifies that W. DEAN BROWN

is the registered holder

of Five Thousand *shares of the above named corporation. This certificate is transferable on the books of the corporation only by the shareholder named herein or by the shareholder's duly appointed representative upon surrender of this certificate properly endorsed. This stock has not been registered with any Federal or State agency and its transfer is subject to restriction. Total authorized issue of this series of stock is* 100,000 *shares with* no *par value. The corporation is organized in The State of* Tennessee

In Witness Whereof, said corporation has caused this Certificate to be signed by its duly authorized officers and its Corporate Seal to be hereunto affixed,

this 3rd *day* *of* April *A.D.* 1999

Seal

Jane Gray

SECRETARY

W. Dean Brown

PRESIDENT

For Value Received, I *hereby sell, assign and transfer unto*

Charles Frost , Five Thousand *shares*

of stock represented by this certificate, and do hereby irrevocably constitute and appoint

Jane Gray *, Corporate Secretary as Agent to transfer*

said shares on the books of the within named corporation with full power of substitution in

the premises.

Dated: 1/21/02

Signature of Shareholder **W. Dean Brown**

Signature of Witness **Jane Gray**

Don't complete the back of this certificate
unless you are selling your stock.

The following abbreviations, when used in the inscription on the face of this certificate, shall be construed as though they were written out in full according to applicable laws or regulations:

TEN COM .... as tenants in common

TEN ENT .... as tenants by the entireties

JT TEN .... as joint tenants with right of survivorship and not as tenants in common

UNIF GIFT MIN ACT:

(Name of Custodian) as Custodian for (Name of Minor) under Uniform Gifts to Minors Act (Name of State)

NUMBER OF SHARES

CERTIFICATE NUMBER

CERTIFICATE OF STOCK

This Certifies that

is the registered holder

of

shares of the above named corporation. This certificate is transferable on the books

of the corporation only by the shareholder named herein or by the shareholder's duly appointed representative upon

surrender of this certificate properly endorsed. This stock has not been registered with any Federal or State agency

and its transfer is subject to restriction. Total authorized issue of this series of stock is

with

par value. The corporation is organized in The State of

shares

In Witness Whereof, said corporation has caused this Certificate to be signed by its duly authorized

officers and its Seal to be hereunto affixed,

this

day

of

A.D.

PRESIDENT

SECRETARY

For Value Received,   *hereby sell, assign and transfer unto*

                       ,   *shares*

of stock represented by this certificate, and do hereby irrevocably constitute and appoint

           , Corporate Secretary as Agent to transfer

said shares on the books of the within named corporation with full power of substitution in

the premises.

Dated:

Signature of Shareholder

Signature of Witness

The following abbreviations, when used in the inscription on the face of this certificate, shall be construed as though they were written out in full according to applicable laws or regulations:

TEN COM .... as tenants in common

TEN ENT .... as tenants by the entireties

JT TEN .... as joint tenants with right of survivorship and not as tenants in common

UNIF GIFT MIN ACT:

(Name of Custodian) as Custodian for (Name of Minor) under Uniform Gifts to Minors Act (Name of State)

NUMBER OF SHARES

CERTIFICATE NUMBER

CERTIFICATE OF STOCK

This Certifies that

_____ is the registered holder of

_____ shares of the above named corporation. This certificate is transferable on the books of the corporation only by the shareholder named herein or by the shareholder's duly appointed representative upon surrender of this certificate properly endorsed. This stock has not been registered with any Federal or State agency and its transfer is subject to restriction. Total authorized issue of this series of stock is _____ shares with _____ par value. The corporation is organized in The State of _____.

In Witness Whereof, said corporation has caused this Certificate to be signed by its duly authorized officers and its Seal to be hereunto affixed,

this _____ day _____ of _____ A. D. _____

PRESIDENT

SECRETARY

For Value Received, hereby sell, assign and transfer unto

, shares

of stock represented by this certificate, and do hereby irrevocably constitute and appoint

, Corporate Secretary as Agent to transfer

said shares on the books of the within named corporation with full power of substitution in the premises.

Dated:

Signature of Shareholder

Signature of Witness

The following abbreviations, when used in the inscription on the face of this certificate, shall be construed as though they were written out in full according to applicable laws or regulations:

TEN COM .... as tenants in common

TEN ENT .... as tenants by the entireties

JT TEN .... as joint tenants with right of survivorship and not as tenants in common

UNIF GIFT MIN ACT:

(Name of Custodian) as Custodian for (Name of Minor) under Uniform Gifts to Minors Act (Name of State)

NUMBER OF SHARES

CERTIFICATE NUMBER

CERTIFICATE OF STOCK

This Certifies that

shares of the above named corporation. This certificate is transferable on the books of the corporation only by the shareholder named herein or by the shareholder's duly appointed representative upon surrender of this certificate properly endorsed. This stock has not been registered with any Federal or State agency and its transfer is subject to restriction. Total authorized issue of this series of stock is shares

with par value. The corporation is organized in The State of

is the registered holder of

In Witness Whereof, said corporation has caused this Certificate to be signed by its duly authorized officers and its Seal to be hereunto affixed,

this   day   of

A.D.

PRESIDENT

SECRETARY

For Value Received,   *hereby sell, assign and transfer unto*

                       ,   *shares*

of stock represented by this certificate, and do hereby irrevocably constitute and appoint

            , Corporate Secretary as Agent to transfer

said shares on the books of the within named corporation with full power of substitution in

the premises.

Dated:

Signature of Shareholder

Signature of Witness

The following abbreviations, when used in the inscription on the face of this certificate, shall be construed as though they were written out in full according to applicable laws or regulations:

TEN COM .... as tenants in common

TEN ENT .... as tenants by the entireties

JT TEN .... as joint tenants with right of survivorship and not as tenants in common

UNIF GIFT MIN ACT:

(Name of Custodian) as Custodian for (Name of Minor) under Uniform Gifts to Minors Act (Name of State)

NUMBER OF SHARES

CERTIFICATE NUMBER

CERTIFICATE OF STOCK

This Certifies that

_____ is the registered holder

of _____ shares of the above named corporation. This certificate is transferable on the books of the corporation only by the shareholder named herein or by the shareholder's duly appointed representative upon surrender of this certificate properly endorsed. This stock has not been registered with any Federal or State agency and its transfer is subject to restriction. Total authorized issue of this series of stock is _____ shares with _____ par value. The corporation is organized in The State of _____.

In Witness Whereof, said corporation has caused this Certificate to be signed by its duly authorized officers and its Seal to be hereunto affixed,

this _____ day of _____ A.D. _____

_____
PRESIDENT

_____
SECRETARY

For Value Received, hereby sell, assign and transfer unto

, shares

of stock represented by this certificate, and do hereby irrevocably constitute and appoint

, Corporate Secretary as Agent to transfer

said shares on the books of the within named corporation with full power of substitution in

the premises.

Dated:

Signature of Shareholder

Signature of Witness

The following abbreviations, when used in the inscription on the face of this certificate, shall be construed as though they were written out in full according to applicable laws or regulations:

TEN COM .... as tenants in common

TEN ENT .... as tenants by the entireties

JT TEN .... as joint tenants with right of survivorship and not as tenants in common

UNIF GIFT MIN ACT:

(Name of Custodian) as Custodian for (Name of Minor) under Uniform Gifts to Minors Act (Name of State)

CERTIFICATE OF STOCK

NUMBER OF SHARES

CERTIFICATE NUMBER

This Certifies that

is the registered holder of

shares of the above named corporation. This certificate is transferable on the books of the corporation only by the shareholder named herein or by the shareholder's duly appointed representative upon surrender of this certificate properly endorsed. This stock has not been registered with any Federal or State agency and its transfer is subject to restriction. Total authorized issue of this series of stock is shares with par value. The corporation is organized in The State of

In Witness Whereof, said corporation has caused this Certificate to be signed by its duly authorized officers and its Seal to be hereunto affixed,

this   day   of   A.D.

_____
PRESIDENT

_____
SECRETARY

For Value Received, hereby sell, assign and transfer unto

,
shares

of stock represented by this certificate, and do hereby irrevocably constitute and appoint

, Corporate Secretary as Agent to transfer

said shares on the books of the within named corporation with full power of substitution in

the premises.

Dated:

Signature of Shareholder

Signature of Witness

The following abbreviations, when used in the inscription on the face of this certificate, shall be construed as though they were written out in full according to applicable laws or regulations:

TEN COM .... as tenants in common

TEN ENT .... as tenants by the entireties

JT TEN .... as joint tenants with right of survivorship and not as tenants in common

UNIF GIFT MIN ACT:

(Name of Custodian) as Custodian for (Name of Minor) under Uniform Gifts to Minors Act (Name of State)

NUMBER OF SHARES

CERTIFICATE NUMBER

CERTIFICATE OF STOCK

This Certifies that _____ is the registered holder

of _____ shares of the above named corporation. This certificate is transferable on the books

of the corporation only by the shareholder named herein or by the shareholders' duly appointed representative upon

surrender of this certificate properly endorsed. This stock has not been registered with any Federal or State agency

and its transfer is subject to restriction. Total authorized issue of this series of stock is _____ shares

with _____ par value. The corporation is organized in The State of _____

In Witness Whereof, said corporation has caused this Certificate to be signed by its duly authorized

officers and its Seal to be hereunto affixed,

this _____ day _____ of _____ A.D.

_____
PRESIDENT

_____
SECRETARY

For Value Received, _____ *hereby sell, assign and transfer unto*

_____ , _____ *shares*

of stock represented by this certificate, and do hereby irrevocably constitute and appoint

_____ *, Corporate Secretary as Agent to transfer*

said shares on the books of the within named corporation with full power of substitution in

the premises.

Dated: _____

Signature of Shareholder _____

Signature of Witness _____

The following abbreviations, when used in the inscription on the face of this certificate, shall be construed as though they were written out in full according to applicable laws or regulations:

TEN COM .... as tenants in common

TEN ENT .... as tenants by the entireties

JT TEN .... as joint tenants with right of survivorship and not as tenants in common

UNIF GIFT MIN ACT:

(Name of Custodian) as Custodian for (Name of Minor) under Uniform Gifts to Minors Act (Name of State)

Forming A Limited Liability Company

Forming a limited liability company is almost identical to forming a corporation. In fact, the only real difference is the terminology used. Everything else including the procedure is basically the same. For example, the form that you file with the state to organize a corporation is called the "Articles of Incorporation." Similarly, the form used to organize a limited liability company is called the "Articles of Organization." They both contain basically the same information - the title is just different.

You'll see some other differences as well. For example, owners of a corporation are known as shareholders, and the owners of limited liability company are termed members. Also, with an LLC, there are no directors or officers. The company is managed directly by the owners. The last major difference is this. Corporations operate by a set of rules called bylaws and the operation of the LLC is governed by an operating agreement.

A little background...

Although many people think the limited liability company is an alternative to the corporation, it was actually conceived as a better alternative to the partnership, especially the limited partnership. Popular in Europe for years, the first LLCs seen in the states were formed in Wyoming and weren't even recognized by other states. Since business owners were leery of this new type of business organization, its popularity suffered until recently. In the last five years, many states have adopted laws that recognize and allow the formation of LLCs within their borders.

of LLCs within their borders.

Why did we need a new type of business organization? The limited liability company came in answer to the demands of the organizers of limited partnerships. A limited partnership is a special type of partnership used for large financing deals - movies, real estate, etc. It consists of one "general" partner who organizes the deal, and one or more "investor" partners. The investor partners enjoy limited liability protection against partnership obligations, but the general partner's exposure is unlimited. The general partner has *no* liability protection. Hence the need for an entity like the LLC which offers limited liability to all partners - even the general partner.

Basically, the LLC offers the limited liability protection of the corporation with the pass-through taxation of the partnership. The S Corporation offers the same benefits, but its 75 (formerly 35) shareholder limit removes it as an option for typical financing deals that consist of hundreds or even thousands of investor partners. (These types of deals are often sold by brokerage firms as investments.) Since they are taxed like a partnership, LLC losses usually generated in the early years offer a tax write-off to the investor, coupled with favorable taxation of the financial rewards at the maturity of the project. A perfect fit for the limited liability company. Perhaps a perfect fit for those starting a real estate investment business where you buy houses, rent them while they appreciate in value, and sell them at some point in the future.

Why the limited liability company is becoming an alternative to the corporation is what I'm still trying to figure out. It was meant to replace the partnership. Perhaps it's due to misinformation or the "newer is better" phenomenon. A limited liability company wasn't designed for any and all businesses. It was designed for a specific type of business - a real estate or investment holding company that requires investment partners. Being taxed like a partnership is not something every business owner wants. Most people don't want income from their business ending up on their personal tax return.

THE ORGANIZATION PROCESS

If you read the corporation chapter, you'll find that the process of organizing a limited liability company is almost identical. Accordingly, the corporation chapter and this one are very similar.

Organizing a limited liability company is very simple and consists of four basic steps, choosing a name, filing a form with the state, attending to some organizational matters like issuing member certificates, and setting up your LLC records book. Please read all of the steps and understand them fully before completing any step. A mistake could result in having to redo and refile paperwork, costing you time and money. The process outlined here is applicable to any state. The last chapter will give attention to any state specific variations of the procedure outlined here.

Step 1.   Choose your company name.
Step 2.   File your paperwork with the state.
Step 3.   Take care of organizational matters.
Step 4.   Prepare a company record book.

Step 1. Choose A Name

The first step in organizing your LLC is selecting a name. Your name must meet specific requirements outlined by State law:

Requirement 1...
The name must show that your company is a limited liability company. It must contain either "A Limited Liability Company" or the abbreviation LLC. This tells the world that you are operating as a limited liability company. This way, other businesses, creditors, etc. know that you are not responsible for company obligations, and that any lawsuits must be brought against the company.

Requirement 2...
The name must be different from the names already on file with the Secretary of State. This includes LLCs, corporations, assumed or fictitious names, out of state corporations doing business in the state, and registered trademarks. Also, your company name may not be "deceptively similar" to other names in use. This keeps companies from benefiting from the goodwill created by another company.

However, if another entity has taken the name you want to use, all you'll need to do is add another word to it to satisfy the requirement. For example, if your last name is Brown and you want to use "Brown, LLC." as your company name, you'll probably find that another entrepreneur named Brown beat you to it. However, you can still use Brown in your company name if you simply add another word or initial. For example, you could name it Brown Ventures, LLC, Brown Publishing, LLC, or Dean Brown, LLC. Oh by the way, changing the identifier doesn't change the name. That is, changing from "LLC" to "Limited Liability Company" doesn't help, "Brown, LLC." and "Brown, A Limited Liability Company" is the same name.

Please note that if you find the name you want to use available according to the records of the Secretary of State, there may still be an unincorporated business like a sole proprietorship or partnership using the name. According to law, the business that uses the name first in a geographic location has the right to use the name. To check for these types of businesses, you can look in the white pages of your telephone directory. If you plan to do business in other cities, you may want to check those telephone directories too. If you want to do business state wide, regionally, or nationally, you may consider having your name researched by professionals and registered as a trademark with the U.S. Patent and Trademark office. Registering a trademark gives you the right to use the name in all 50 states. For more information on trademarks, see the book entitled "Trademarks, How to Name Your Business & Product" in the catalog at the back of the book.

Requirement 3…

The company name may not contain a word or phrase indicating that it's organized to transact business for which it has not been approved. For example, your company name can't contain the word "insurance" unless the company has satisfied state requirements for organizing as an insurance company. The same applies for other types of regulated businesses like banks, investment firms, physicians, accountants, etc.

Also, the name may not imply that the it's affiliated with or sponsored by any fraternal, veteran's, service, religious, charitable, or professional organization unless the authorization is officially granted to the business and the authorization is certified in writing. For example, if you're not part of the YMCA, don't include "YMCA" in your company name. In addition, stay away from names that make your company sound like it's a part of the State or Federal government. Although using the word federal in your name is usually okay, be careful not to imply any governmental authority or affiliation.

Other considerations for choosing a name…

Assumed names, fictitious names and DBAs - An assumed name, sometimes called a fictitious name, is a feature of some state laws that allows a business to operate under more than one name. This can be quite convenient to the small business person who operates different businesses but does not want to have several LLCs. Using an assumed name, most people name the LLC something non-identifying like their last name, for example, Jones Inc. They might then name their different companies to be more descriptive of separate product lines, like Quantum Computers LLC, and Standard Computer Software LLC. All of these would simply be different names or aliases for the same company that has only one set of books and the same owners. To let the world know that the company "Jones LLC" and these other companies are the same, a notice to this effect is filed with a state or local official. We'll discuss this further in the last chapter.

Checking the availability of a name...

Since you can't use a name already taken by another entity, documents submitted with a name already in use will be rejected. So, before filing your articles of organization, you'll want to check to see if another business is already using the name. In most states you can find out if "your" name is available by simply calling the Secretary of State and checking. If name checks are available by phone, the telephone number will be listed in the last chapter.

Before you call, be sure of the name you wish to use, and that it contains either "LLC" or "A Limited Liability Company." You should have one or two additional names chosen in case your first choice is not available. Checking your name should only take a couple of minutes. This is a good time to ask any questions you may have and double check the filing fees, etc.

The Secretary of State has computer access to all registered names being used in the state. The role playing outlined below is designed for a telephone call, but of course face to face conversation will be the same. The conversation will basically go like this:

S/S: *Secretary of State's Office, may I help you?*

YOU: *Yes. I'd like to check the availability of a name please. (The person will either check the name, or transfer you to the person who will.)*

S/S: *Okay. What is the name you'd like to check?*

YOU: *Brown Publishing, LLC.*
(The person will now check their computer for the name.)

S/S: *That name appears to be available. (That's great.)*

The Secretary of State will usually only say something like the "name appears to be available." That's because someone may walk into their office five minutes later and file paperwork using "your" name. There are no guarantees as to the availability of a name until your articles of organization is accepted.

If your first choice for a name is already being used, the conversation will continue like this:

S/S: *That name does not appear to be available at this time. Are there any other names you'd like to check? (This is when your second and third choices come in handy.)*

YOU: *Yes. What about Brown Communications, LLC.?*

S/S: *(The person will now check for the new name.) That name does appear to be available at this time. (Yea!)*

If name checks by phone are not offered in this state, you'll have to go ahead and file your articles and hope for the best. If the name you like is already being used, the state will either fax, call, or write you with this information.

Step 3. File Your Paperwork

The paperwork you must file to form a limited liability company is a document called the "Articles Of Organization." Some states require that you file another document or two with the articles but we'll cover that in the last chapter. The articles are easy to complete if you know basic information like your name, the business name, and your address. The document usually provides information about five items, the company; the members or owners; the registered agent; and finally the organizers. The document on the next page is a typical articles of organization. The articles or organization that you will use is in the last chapter.

Completing the articles of organization is pretty simple. Be sure to type the form so it can be accurately recorded by the Secretary of State. (Most states require that the articles be typed.) If you want to type the articles on your computer instead of using a typewriter, the forms in this book are available on a computer disk for IBM PC (Windows) or Mac compatible computers. Now, let's go through the articles of organization one article at a time.

Article 1. Name...
This one is pretty simple. Just put your company name here. Make sure the name meets state requirements and includes an identifier like "LLC."

Article 2. Office...
Another easy one. Include here the street address of the corporation's principle office. Your home address is okay to use.

Example

ARTICLES OF ORGANIZATION

Pursuant to Article 2.01 of the Texas Limited Liability Company Act, the undersigned incorporator submits these articles of organization for the purpose of forming a limited liability company.

Article 1. The name of the limited liability company is:

Consumer Publishing, LLC

Article 2. The principal office of the limited liability company is located at:

1234 Main Street, Houston, TX 12345

Article 3. The company's period of duration is perpetual.

Article 4. The management of the company is reserved to the members. The name and address of its initial member is:

Dean Brown 1234 Main Street, Houston, TX 12345

Article 5. The purpose or purposes for which the corporation is organized is to engage in any lawful act or activity allowed by Texas Limited Liability Company Act.

Article 6. The name of the corporation's registered agent, and the street address of the corporation's registered office is:

Dean Brown 1234 Main Street, Houston, TX 12345

Article 7. The name and street address of the sole organizer or of this limited liability company is:

Dean Brown 1234 Main Street, Houston, TX 12345

Optional Items:

The effective date of this filing is January 1, 1999.

In witness whereof, the undersigned organizer has executed these Articles of Organization on the date below. The undersigned incorporator hereby declares, under penalty of perjury, that the statements made in the forgoing document are true, and that the organizer is at least eighteen years of age.

Date: November 11, 1998

Signature of Organizer : *Dean Brown*

Article 3. Duration...

The duration of the company is simply how long it will exist. If you are using the company to pursue a single project, you may wish to limit its life-span to the length of the project. Most businesses don't have a particular life-span. Most exist until they go out of business or the sole owner dies. In this case, the life of the company is said to be perpetual, or never ending. Unless you're developing an investment property or have a project with a specific life, the period of duration should be perpetual.

Article 4. Management...

A limited liability company can either be managed by a few appointed members, or by all of the members. If the company is managed by only a few of the members, it is referred to as being "manager-managed." If it is managed by all of the members, it is "member managed." A limited liability company that is manager managed is typical of investment companies. This way, the day-to-day operations of the business can be handled by the managers and the rest of the members need not be involved. This arrangement is typical for investment deals where the organizers run the business as managers and the other members simply provide the investment capital. Member managed is the typical choice for small business people who use the LLC to operate a "regular" business. The forms in this book are designed for a member managed limited liability company.

Article 5. Purpose...

Some states require a purpose clause for your limited liability company. A purpose clause simply states the company's principal business. Once upon a time, you had to specifically state what type of business you were going to operate, but most states now accept the "general purpose clause" shown here. Using this clause, you can operate any type of business that you choose. This clause will also allow you to change the type of business your company transacts as you need.

Article 6. Registered agent...

An LLC's registered agent is the person appointed to accept legal documents on behalf of the company. If someone sues you, the papers will be served on the registered agent at the "registered office." Therefore, a registered agent, sometimes called a resident agent, must be at least 18 years of age and have a street address. You can be your own registered agent, and even use your home address. If you choose to organize in a state where you do not have an office, you will need the services of a registered agent service company. Consumer Publishing can serve as your registered agent in Tennessee or Nevada.

Article 7. Organizer...

The organizer is simply the person who files the articles of organization with the state.

Optional items...

You can include many different items in your articles that are not required provided they are not prohibited by state law. This can include items regarding the management or operation of the company that you need to make a matter of public information.

Delayed effective date - If you are organizing your LLC near the end of the year, you may want to include a delayed effective date of organization. For example, if you are forming your LLC in the month of December, and you aren't going to begin operations until the first of the year, you can include a statement in your articles that states the filing won't be effective until January first. This way, you won't have to file any tax returns for this "short" tax year beginning in December. State and Federal agencies won't be expecting you to be open for business until the first of January. To make sure the Secretary of State sees this, put a yellow Post-it(r) Note on the articles that says: "Notice-delayed effective date."

All those involved do not need to sign the articles of organization. Only the person completing the articles of organization (the organizer) needs to sign. Now you are ready to file your articles. You can either mail, send them by overnight courier, or take them to the secretary of state's office yourself.

Step 3. Take care of Organizational Matters

After your articles of organization are filed, you'll need to tend to a few other details before the formation of your limited liability company is complete. Primarily, you need to prepare and/or adopt an operating agreement and issue member certificates.

An operating agreement is simply an agreement between the members of the LLC as to how the company will be operated. It spells out things like voting rights and how profits will be distributed. At the end of this chapter a typical operating agreement is provided for your use. You can either use it as is, or modify it for your own particular use. The documents contained in this book, including the operating agreement, are available on a computer disk. The disk is available for PC (Windows) or Macintosh computers.

The operating agreement...

At the end of this chapter, you'll find a standard limited liability company operating agreement. You can either use it as it is, or make modifications to suit your particular needs. If you decide to use it as it is, all you'll need to do is fill in the blanks for date, company name, officers, and members. Then have each member sign it, give a copy to each member, and place the original in the company record book.

Remember that giving property for your LLC interest may give rise to tax problems. It's usually best to simply give cash for your ownership interest and then sell or lease the property to the company. This way you can receive lease payments from the company for its use, making it lease or rental income to you. This is a good way to get money out of the company without paying Social Security taxes. (Rental income is only subject to regular income taxes.) One word of caution here, be careful when leasing vehicles or dangerous equipment to the company. If someone gets injured by the vehicle or equipment, the injured party may try to recover from you as the lessor of the equipment.

Member certificates...

Member certificates for an LLC are like stock certificates for a corporation. They are issued to each member as evidence of ownership in the company. All you need to do to issue certificates is follow the example. Each certificate should be sequentially numbered, that is 01,02,03, etc. The member's name and ownership percentage must be shown. The certificate is signed by the president and secretary of the company.

Step 4. Prepare a Company Record Book

Although a limited liability company is not required to have scheduled meetings like a corporation, you will hold unscheduled meetings from time to time to discuss matters relating to the company. You will need to keep minutes of these meetings and keep them organized. Properly organized records are one of the first things the IRS will ask to see if you ever get audited. Also, if you intent to seek financing for your new venture, your banker will want to see your records. Although you can organize them in any convenient manner, a lot of people use a Limited Liability Company Record Book for storing their records. A Record Book is simply a nice binder with divided sections for storing your company documents, minutes, and certificates.

Your company minute book can be as simple as a three ring indexed binder or a fully customized outfit with an engraved seal. In preparing a record book, you have two choices, either prepare your own, or purchase one.

Purchase one...

If you choose to purchase one and are unable to find a local supplier, LLC minute books and seals are available through Consumer Publishing. Our kits are the same as those used by attorneys. You can either use your credit card and order by calling 1-800-677-2462, or send a check with the order form in the back of the book. Outfits are shipped within 24 hours, and next day service is also available.

Each limited liability outfit includes:

- *A deluxe binder with the company name gold embossed on the spine,*
- *A matching slip case to protect your records from dust,*
- *An seal engraved with your company name for embossing membership certificates and contracts,*
- *20 Member Certificates imprinted with the company name,*
- *A membership certificate transfer ledger,*
- *Preprinted minutes and operating agreement,*
- *Member meeting forms.*

Make your own...

If you prefer to prepare your own record book, you'll need to visit a legal stationary or lawyer supply store and purchase the following:

- *A three ring binder,*
- *At least 7 tabbed index dividers to divide the book into sections,*
- *Pre-punched three ring binder paper to keep minutes on,*
- *A limited liability company seal.*

A seal should be included with the record book because the seal is how the company "signs" contracts, minutes, and other official documents like member certificates. The seal is maintained by the company secretary and is used to show that the company approves of documents that the seal is applied to.

After you have all of your supplies together, you should assemble them as follows.

1. *Prepare these headings for the tabbed index dividers; APPLICATIONS & PERMITS; STATE FILINGS; OPERATING AGREEMENT; MINUTES; MEMBER CERTIFICATES; FORMS; and TRANSFER LEDGER.*

2. *Three hole punch the documents already filed with the state and/or the IRS, as well as the completed meeting minutes and insert them into the appropriate sections of the record book.*

3. *Copy or remove the operating agreement from this chapter and insert it into the appropriate section.*

4. *Place any minutes taken into the minute section.*

5. *Prepare a separate list of members and officers, of the company and include them in the TRANSFER LEDGER section. Be sure to update these lists if anything changes.*

Record keeping...

Below is a list of the records you should keep for your company. These records must be available for member inspection and should be kept at the company offices.

- *Minutes of all member meetings, generally for the last 3 years.*
- *Appropriate accounting records and financial reports.*
- *An alphabetical list of all members and their addresses.*
- *An alphabetical list of all officers with their business addresses.*
- *Copies of all formal documents used to organize the business.*
- *All written communications to members for the past 3 years.*
- *Financial statements for the past 3 years.*
- *A copy of the most recent annual report.*
- *All contracts entered into by the company.*
- *Amendments to, or changes in the operating agreement.*
- *Records of member certificate issues and transfers.*
- *Promissory notes.*
- *Life insurance policies held on company officers.*

Holding meetings...

You will remember that the company is a separate "person" that cannot physically act for itself, so it acts through its members and officers. Whenever members meet to discuss and decide what actions the company will take, the meeting, and what was discussed, must be documented on paper. This documentation is known as the minutes of the meeting.

The documentation of meetings and even the meeting itself need not be made over formalized. For example, many people formally call the meeting to order; formally ask for turns to speak; formally make, and second motions; and formally adjourn the meeting. This formality comes from meetings of large corporations, and is not necessary for small LLC meetings, so don't get caught in this overly structured form.

When holding a meeting, all you need to do is sit down, discuss what needs to be done, vote on the matter, summarize it on paper, and have everyone sign it. The best way to do this is to write down everything that happens on a plain piece of paper, summarize, and organize the information later, then transfer it to a formal minutes type form. Blank minute sheets for your use are included in minute books that we offer and on our available computer disk.

You're Done

This completes the organization of your limited liability company. On the next few pages, you'll find a standard operating agreement and member certificates for your use. The articles of organization for your use is in the last chapter.

OPERATING AGREEMENT

(Member Managed Limited Liability Company)

The following document is the operating agreement of :

hereafter referred to in this document as "The Company."

    The Company was formed on   when articles of organization were filed with the state of   . A copy of this document has been placed in The Company record book. All members of The Company hereby agree with its provisions. The Company will be managed by its member(s).

GENERAL PROVISIONS

Ownership Percentage - A member's ownership interest in The Company shall be calculated as a percentage based on the member's capital contribution. A member's "ownership percentage" shall the calculated as follows: the members capital contribution divided by total contributed capital shown on the books of The Company. Transfer of a member's ownership of The Company, or a change in a member's ownership percentage in The company may only take place upon approval of a majority of the members.

Voting - Each member shall be entitled to vote on matters affecting The Company at a meeting held to discuss such matters. A member's voting "power" shall be equal to the member's ownership percentage as calculated above. Any matter brought before the members to be voted on shall pass when approved by more than 50% of the members as based on their ownership percentage.

Compensation - Members will not be paid for their time in managing The Company. Members may, however, receive compensation in the form of salaries, bonuses, or any other gratuity allowed by law for services rendered to The Company as an employee, officer, or independent contractor. Also, members may be reimbursed for reasonable expenses incurred on behalf of The Company as evidenced by proper receipts.

Other Business Interests - A member may not own or be involved in any way with an activity or entity that competes with The Company, or otherwise might diminish the earning potential of The Company without the prior written approval of all members.

Meetings - At this time, The Company does not have scheduled meetings, but it may provide for such scheduled meetings upon the approval of a majority of members. A special meeting may be requested by a member at any time either verbally or in writing. The member making this call for a meeting shall provide a proposed date and time for the meeting. Agreement to have a meeting can be expressed by the members either verbally or in witting. If any member can not attend the meeting, then the member(s) unable to attend shall propose an alternative date and time for the meeting.

If all the members cannot attend the proposed meeting, then it shall be postponed until all members can attend. A requested meeting may not be postponed for more than six months. A meeting of The Company may be held without all members in attendance if the member(s) unable to attend provide in writing their approval of the meeting.

Minutes of all meetings shall be taken and a copy provided to all members. A copy shall also be placed in The Company minute book.

Membership Certificates - The Company shall provide membership certificates to each member, a sample of which shall be attached to this agreement. Each membership certificate shall be sequentially numbered and reflect the member's ownership percentage. It shall also bear the name of The Company and the name of the member. It shall be signed and dated by The Company's duly appointed secretary as provided in this agreement.

FINANCIAL PROVISIONS

Tax Classification - The members intend for The Company to be taxed as a partnership. Officers are hereby granted authority to do whatever necessary to retain "partnership" tax status with State and Federal agencies.

Accounting - The Company shall have a tax year beginning January 1 and ending December 31 of each year. Accordingly, The Company shall be known as a calendar year taxpayer. The books of The Company shall be maintained on a cash basis with income being recognized when it is received, and expenses recognized when they are paid.

Tax Matters Partner - The Company shall appoint a representative to handle tax and accounting matters. This person shall be the Secretary of The Company, and if the Secretary is unable to act in this position, then the President shall act instead.

Banking - The President and Secretary of The Company shall establish bank account(s) with a bank that meets the approval of all members. The President and Secretary shall sign on the account and have the authority to draft funds from said accounts for payment of company obligations. No officer of The Company shall have the authority to borrow money or obtain lines of credit without express written approval of all members. This does not, however, apply to credit accounts opened with suppliers. The officers may obtain credit from suppliers in due course of operating the business. Bank statements shall be available to all members at any time upon their request either verbally or in writing.

Property - Title to all property purchased or leased for The Company shall be titled in the name of The Company. Officers are hereby granted authority lease equipment on behalf of The Company in due course of business.

Capital Contributions - In consideration for their percentage ownership in The Company, members shall contribute either cash, property, or services to The Company. Cash received shall be deposited in The Company's bank account and no interest shall be paid on the amount. Title to any property given shall be transferred to The Company. Below is an accounting of consideration given by the members in exchange for their ownership in The Company.

Name	Consideration Given	Value	Ownership %

Members may decide occasionally that additional capital must be contributed to The Company. This decision shall be made at a meeting of the members with all members in attendance. Since any change in the capital accounts will result in a change in the ownership percentage, the decision must be unanimous.

Capital Withdrawals - Members are not allowed to withdraw their capital contributions without written approval of all members. Members will not be able to "Draw" against their capital contributions without written approval of all members. Loans to members may be approved form time to time as circumstances arise. Loans must be approved by all members.

Distributions - From time to time distributions may be made from profits, sale of equipment, or other sources. Before payment, distributions shall be approved by all members and shall be paid to each member in proportion to their ownership percentage. In the event that The Company ceases operations, distributions of cash and property shall be made to the members after all creditors and suppliers are paid. Such a distribution shall be made to the members in proportion to their ownership percentage.

OWNERSHIP

Changes In Ownership - A member can withdraw from The Company at any time. The member wanting to withdraw must give written notice to the other members 60 days prior to the date of withdrawal.

Transfer of Membership - A member may not transfer, sell, assign, offer as collateral, or pledge his/her ownership in The Company without prior written approval of the other members. This transfer restriction also applies to the members voting rights.

DISSOLUTION

The Company shall be dissolved upon any of the following events:

- Death or other event that prevents a member from participating in the operation of The company. In this event, the remaining members may vote not to dissolve The Company within 90 days. If the remaining members agree unanimously, The Company shall continue and not dissolve.

- Agreement of all members to dissolve The Company

OTHER PROVISIONS

Officers - Members may agree to appoint one or more officers to be responsible for representing The Company in its due course of business. It is agreed to appoint at least a President and a Secretary. Other offices and officers may be appointed as the need arises or at the pleasure of the members. Officers may be compensated for services rendered in their respective positions. This compensation may be in addition to any other compensation received from The Company. The following members shall be officers of the company:

President _____

Secretary _____

Company Records - The Company Secretary must maintain all records for The Company that are required by law. This may include but not be limited to a list of all members including their addresses and ownership percentage, records of ownership transfers, minutes of all member meetings, bank statements and accounting records. These records are to be kept at the principal office of The Company and may be reviewed by any member by giving at least one day's notice to The Company's Secretary.

Authority - Officers of The Company and or any member of The Company has authority to transact any business or enter into any transaction or carry out any act to complete the formation of the Company or further its financial interest in the due course of business with one exception: No member has authority to obtain loans, lines of credit or commit The Company to any bank or lending institution without prior written approval of all members.

Disputes - In the event of a dispute between the members regarding this operating agreement or any matter regarding The Company, the dispute shall be settled by arbitration according to the rules of the American Arbitration Association. The arbitration or mediation service hearing the dispute shall be agreed upon by the members before proceeding. The cost of the arbitration/mediation shall be borne by The company.

If the dispute cannot be settled by arbitration, the matter may go to before a court with jurisdiction in such matters. If the matter goes before a court, then the members individually shall bear the cost of the proceedings. The prevailing party may seek reimbursement of expenses related to the proceedings.

Changes - This document is the only agreement between the members of The Company and replaces any verbal or written agreement between members. It cannot be replaced, amended or altered in any way without the approval of the members of The Company that adopted and approved the agreement being replaced or amended. If any provision of this agreement is determined to be legally unenforceable, then that provision only shall be stricken from the agreement, leaving the remainder of the agreement in force.

As evidenced by their signatures below, the members hereby adopt this agreement in its entirety and agree to bound by its terms. The signatures need not be notarized.

Date _____

_____

_____

_____

_____

_____

_____

Example **MEMBER CERTIFICATE**

CONSUMER PUBLISHING LLC

This Certifies that W. DEAN BROWN is the registered holder of - FIFTY - percent of the above named *Limited Liability Company* and is entitled to the rights and privileges of membership therein, and subject to the duties and obligations of membership as outlined in the *Company's Operating Agreement.* The issuance of this certificate has not been registered with any State or Federal agency and its transfer is subject to restriction. This certificate is transferable on the books of the company only by the member named herein or by the members duly appointed representative upon surrender of this certificate properly endorsed. This *Limited Liability Company* is organized in *The State of* Tennessee .

In Witness Whereof, said company has caused this Certificate to be signed by its duly authorized officers and its Company Seal to be hereunto affixed,

this 3rd day of April A.D. 1999

Seal

Jane Gray

SECRETARY

W. Dean Brown

PRESIDENT

For Value Received, I *hereby sell, assign and transfer unto*

Charles Frost , Fifty *percent*

ownership in the Limited Liability Company named on the face of this certificate,
and do hereby irrevocably constitute and appoint Jane Gray *, Company*
Secretary as Agent to transfer said ownership on the books of the within named Com-
pany with full power of substitution in the premises.

Dated: 1/21/02

Signature of Member **W. Dean Brown**

Signature of Witness **Jane Gray**

> *Don't complete the back of this certificate*
> *unless you are selling your membership.*

The following abbreviations, when used in the inscription on the face of this certificate, shall be construed as though they were written out in full according to applicable laws or regulations:

TEN COM .... as tenants in common

TEN ENT .... as tenants by the entireties

JT TEN .... as joint tenants with right of survivorship and not as tenants in common

UNIF GIFT MIN ACT:

(Name of Custodian) as Custodian for (Name of Minor) under Uniform Gifts to Minors Act (Name of State)

PERCENTAGE OWNERSHIP

CERTIFICATE NUMBER

MEMBERSHIP CERTIFICATE

This Certifies that _____ is the registered holder of _____ percent of the above named *Limited Liability Company* and is entitled to the rights and privileges of membership therein, and subject to the duties and obligations of membership as outlined in the *Company's Operating Agreement*. The issuance of this certificate has not been registered with any *State* or *Federal agency* and its transfer is subject to restriction. This certificate is transferable on the books of the company only by the member named herein or by the member's duly appointed representative upon surrender of this certificate properly endorsed. This *Limited Liability Company* is organized in *The State of* _____ .

In Witness Whereof, said company has caused this *Certificate* to be signed by its duly authorized officers and its *Seal* to be hereunto affixed,

this _____ day _____ of _____ A.D. _____

_____
SECRETARY

_____
PRESIDENT

For Value Received, hereby sell, assign and transfer unto

, percent

ownership in the Limited Liability Company named on the face of this certificate, and do hereby irrevocably constitute and appoint , Company Secretary as Agent to transfer said ownership on the books of the within named Company with full power of substitution in the premises.

Dated:

Signature of Member

Signature of Witness

The following abbreviations, when used in the inscription on the face of this certificate, shall be construed as though they were written out in full according to applicable laws or regulations:

TEN COM .... as tenants in common

TEN ENT .... as tenants by the entireties

JT TEN .... as joint tenants with right of survivorship and not as tenants in common

UNIF GIFT MIN ACT:

(Name of Custodian) as Custodian for (Name of Minor) under Uniform Gifts to Minors Act (Name of State)

MEMBERSHIP CERTIFICATE

PERCENTAGE OWNERSHIP

CERTIFICATE NUMBER

This Certifies that _____ is the registered holder

of _____ percent of the above named *Limited Liability Company* and is entitled to

the rights and privileges of membership therein, and subject to the duties and obligations of membership as outlined in

the *Company's Operating Agreement*. The issuance of this certificate has not been registered with any State or

Federal agency and its transfer is subject to restriction. This certificate is transferable on the books of the company

only by the member named herein or by the member's duly appointed representative upon surrender of this certificate

properly endorsed. This *Limited Liability Company* is organized in The State of _____ .

In Witness Whereof, said company has caused this *Certificate* to be signed by its duly authorized

officers and its Seal to be hereunto affixed,

this _____ day of _____ *A.D.* _____

_____
PRESIDENT

_____
SECRETARY

For Value Received,   *hereby sell, assign and transfer unto*

       ,   *percent*

ownership in the Limited Liability Company named on the face of this certificate,
and do hereby irrevocably constitute and appoint   *, Company*
Secretary as Agent to transfer said ownership on the books of the within named Com-
pany with full power of substitution in the premises.

Dated:

Signature of Member

Signature of Witness

The following abbreviations, when used in the inscription on the face of this certificate, shall be construed as though they were written out in full according to applicable laws or regulations:

TEN COM .... as tenants in common

TEN ENT .... as tenants by the entireties

JT TEN .... as joint tenants with right of survivorship and not as tenants in common

UNIF GIFT MIN ACT:

(Name of Custodian) as Custodian for (Name of Minor) under Uniform Gifts to Minors Act (Name of State)

PERCENTAGE OWNERSHIP

CERTIFICATE NUMBER

MEMBERSHIP CERTIFICATE

This Certifies that _____ is the registered holder

of _____ percent of the above named *Limited Liability Company* and is entitled to

the rights and privileges of membership therein, and subject to the duties and obligations of membership as outlined in

the *Company's Operating Agreement.* The issuance of this certificate has not been registered with any *State* or

Federal agency and its transfer is subject to restriction. This certificate is transferable on the books of the company

only by the member named herein or by the member's duly appointed representative upon surrender of this certificate

properly endorsed. This *Limited Liability Company* is organized in *The State of* _____ .

In Witness Whereof, said company has caused this *Certificate* to be signed by its duly authorized

officers and its Seal to be hereunto affixed,

this _____ day _____ of _____ *A.D.* _____

_____
SECRETARY

_____
PRESIDENT

For Value Received, hereby sell, assign and transfer unto

, percent

ownership in the *Limited Liability Company* named on the face of this certificate, and do hereby irrevocably constitute and appoint , Company Secretary as Agent to transfer said ownership on the books of the within named Company with full power of substitution in the premises.

Dated:

Signature of Member

Signature of Witness

The following abbreviations, when used in the inscription on the face of this certificate, shall be construed as though they were written out in full according to applicable laws or regulations:

TEN COM .... as tenants in common

TEN ENT .... as tenants by the entireties

JT TEN .... as joint tenants with right of survivorship and not as tenants in common

UNIF GIFT MIN ACT:

(Name of Custodian) as Custodian for (Name of Minor) under Uniform Gifts to Minors Act (Name of State)

MEMBERSHIP CERTIFICATE

PERCENTAGE OWNERSHIP

CERTIFICATE NUMBER

This Certifies that _____ is the registered holder of _____ percent of the above named *Limited Liability Company* and is entitled to the rights and privileges of membership therein, and subject to the duties and obligations of membership as outlined in the Company's Operating Agreement. The issuance of this certificate has not been registered with any State or Federal agency and its transfer is subject to restriction. This certificate is transferable on the books of the company only by the member named herein or by the member's duly appointed representative upon surrender of this certificate properly endorsed. This Limited Liability Company is organized in The State of _____.

In Witness Whereof, said company has caused this Certificate to be signed by its duly authorized officers and its Seal to be hereunto affixed, this _____ day _____ of _____ A.D. _____

_____
SECRETARY

_____
PRESIDENT

For Value Received, hereby sell, assign and transfer unto

, percent

ownership in the Limited Liability Company named on the face of this certificate, and do hereby irrevocably constitute and appoint , Company Secretary as Agent to transfer said ownership on the books of the within named Company with full power of substitution in the premises.

Dated:

Signature of Member

Signature of Witness

The following abbreviations, when used in the inscription on the face of this certificate, shall be construed as though they were written out in full according to applicable laws or regulations:

TEN COM .... as tenants in common

TEN ENT .... as tenants by the entireties

JT TEN .... as joint tenants with right of survivorship and not as tenants in common

UNIF GIFT MIN ACT:

(Name of Custodian) as Custodian for (Name of Minor) under Uniform Gifts to Minors Act (Name of State)

MEMBERSHIP CERTIFICATE

This Certifies that _____ is the registered holder

of _____ percent of the above named *Limited Liability Company* and is entitled to

the rights and privileges of membership therein, and subject to the duties and obligations of membership as outlined in

the *Company's Operating Agreement.* The issuance of this certificate has not been registered with any State or

Federal agency and its transfer is subject to restriction. This certificate is transferable on the books of the company

only by the member named herein or by the member's duly appointed representative upon surrender of this certificate

properly endorsed. This *Limited Liability Company* is organized in The State of _____ .

In Witness Whereof, said company has caused this *Certificate* to be signed by its duly authorized

officers and its Seal to be hereunto affixed,

this _____ day _____ of _____ A. D. _____

_____
PRESIDENT

_____
SECRETARY

For Value Received,   *hereby sell, assign and transfer unto*

           ,   *percent*

ownership in the Limited Liability Company named on the face of this certificate, and do hereby irrevocably constitute and appoint   *, Company Secretary as Agent to transfer said ownership on the books of the within named Company with full power of substitution in the premises.*

Dated:

Signature of Member

Signature of Witness

The following abbreviations, when used in the inscription on the face of this certificate, shall be construed as though they were written out in full according to applicable laws or regulations:

TEN COM .... as tenants in common

TEN ENT .... as tenants by the entireties

JT TEN .... as joint tenants with right of survivorship and not as tenants in common

UNIF GIFT MIN ACT:

(Name of Custodian) as Custodian for (Name of Minor) under Uniform Gifts to Minors Act (Name of State)

PERCENTAGE OWNERSHIP

CERTIFICATE NUMBER

MEMBERSHIP CERTIFICATE

This Certifies that _____ is the registered holder

of _____ percent of the above named *Limited Liability Company* and is entitled to

the rights and privileges of membership therein, and subject to the duties and obligations of membership as outlined in

the *Company's Operating Agreement*. The issuance of this certificate has not been registered with any State or

Federal agency and its transfer is subject to restriction. This certificate is transferable on the books of the company

only by the member named herein or by the member's duly appointed representative upon surrender of this certificate

properly endorsed. This *Limited Liability Company* is organized in *The State of* _____ .

In Witness Whereof, said company has caused this *Certificate to be signed by its duly authorized*

officers and its Seal to be hereunto affixed,

this _____ day _____ of _____ A. D. _____

_____
PRESIDENT

_____
SECRETARY

For Value Received,   *hereby sell, assign and transfer unto*

        ,   *percent*

ownership in the Limited Liability Company named on the face of this certificate, and do hereby irrevocably constitute and appoint   *, Company Secretary as Agent to transfer said ownership on the books of the within named Company with full power of substitution in the premises.*

Dated:

Signature of Member

Signature of Witness

The following abbreviations, when used in the inscription on the face of this certificate, shall be construed as though they were written out in full according to applicable laws or regulations:

TEN COM .... as tenants in common

TEN ENT .... as tenants by the entireties

JT TEN .... as joint tenants with right of survivorship and not as tenants in common

UNIF GIFT MIN ACT:

(Name of Custodian) as Custodian for (Name of Minor) under Uniform Gifts to Minors Act (Name of State)

Forming A Partnership

Of the three types of business organizations covered in this book, the process of forming a partnership is the simplest. Basically all you need to do when forming a partnership is choose a name and write a partnership agreement. There are no state filings, no articles of incorporation, etc.

A partnership agreement is an agreement between the partners that documents how the partners have agreed to operate the partnership. It dictates items like the responsibility and authority of each partner, how monies will be divided, and how ownership is divided. This agreement is not required to be written. It can be simply an oral understanding between the partners - but beware. An unwritten agreement is the making of a disagreement. It is best to have a written partnership agreement.

On the following pages, you will find a standard partnership agreement. You can either use it as is, or make changes to suit your particular needs. To make editing easier, all the forms in this book are available on a computer disk.

Although partnerships are pretty basic and I don't think they need a lot of explanation, there are entire books written about them. If you want to know more about partnerships, you may want to take a look at the book entitled "The Partnership Book" listed in our brochure.

THE ORGANIZATION PROCESS

Organizing a partnership is simple and consists of two basic steps, choosing a name and writing or adopting a partnership agreement.

> *Step 1. Choose your partnership name.*
> *Step 2. Write or adopt a partnership agreement*
> *Step 3. Take care of general business requirements*

Choosing a Name...

Most partnerships are named after their partners. If two partners with the last names Brown and Jones formed a partnership, it would be called "Brown & Jones" and this name would appear on their partnership agreement. Although CPA firms, law firms and other professional firms typically use the partnership name as their business name, a partnership operating a "regular" business probably wouldn't. This type of business, a retail store for example, would want to have a name more descriptive of the business. That's where DBA's come in handy. Sometimes called a "fictitious" or "assumed" name, a DBA (doing business as) allows a partnership to present itself to the public by a name other than the partnership name. Using a fictitious name, the partnership of Brown & Jones, a children's book publisher, could be known as "Kids Press" or something like that. So that everyone knows that Kids Press is actually Brown & Jones, a partnership, Brown & Jones will file a fictitious name statement with a public official in their state. (This is covered in the last chapter.)

Completing The Partnership Agreement...

Completing the partnership agreement is simple. All you have to do is fill in the blanks with required information, have each partner sign the agreement, and give each partner a copy.

After organizing your partnership by adopting your partnership agreement, you'll need to do a few other things before commencing business, things like registering your business name and getting a business permit. We will cover these items in chapter five.

PARTNERSHIP AGREEMENT

The following document is the partnership agreement of :

hereafter referred to in this document as "The Partnership."

The Partnership and its assets will be owned equally by the partners. It is formed by the following individuals:

The Partnership is formed on the date below as signed by the partners, and will continue until it is either dissolved by the partners, a partner leaves, or a partner dies.

Purpose - The purpose of The Partnership is to operate a business, that business being:

Contributions - To provide capital necessary to start the business, the partners have contributed the following property and cash considerations:

Name   Property Value   Cash Contribution

Cash amounts will be deposited in the partnership bank account as soon as it is opened. Interest will not be paid on amounts contributed. If any partner fails to transfer the above funds and or property to the partnership within 60 days of the date below, the partnership will immediately dissolve. In which case, the assets that were transferred to the partnership will be returned to the individuals who contributed them. Additional capital contributions may be made as needed upon agreement of all the partners.

Allocation of Profit or Loss - Profits and losses from the partnership will be shared as shown below. All profits may not be distributed, as profits may be retained by The Partnership to provide for future business needs. The amount of the distribution will be agreed upon by all partners.

Name   %

Partners may "draw" against their share of profits as agreed by a vote of the partners. The Partners may receive compensation in the form of salaries, bonuses, or any other gratuity allowed by law for services rendered to The Partnership as an employee. Also, Partners may be reimbursed for reasonable expenses incurred on behalf of The Partnership as evidenced by proper receipts.

MANAGEMENT

Participation - All partners will actively participate in the business, and share equally in management decisions. A partner may not own or be involved in any way with an activity or entity that competes with The Partnership, or otherwise might diminish the earning potential of The Partnership without the prior written approval of all partners.

Authority - Decisions on behalf of the partnership must be made by unanimous decision of all partners. No partner may, without approval of all the partners, borrow money in the partnership name, sell or otherwise transfer any partnership property, settle any claim for less than what is owed to the partnership, or offer any partnership property as collateral, except in the due course of business,

Meetings - Although the Partnership does not have scheduled meetings, a special meeting may be requested by a partner at any time either verbally or in witting. The partner making this call for a meeting shall provide a proposed date and time for the meeting. Agreement to have a meeting can be expressed by the partners either verbally or in witting. If any partner cannot attend the meeting, then the member(s) unable to attend shall propose an alternative date and time for the meeting.

If all the partners cannot attend the proposed meeting, then it shall be postponed until all partners can attend. A requested meeting may not be postponed for more than six months. A meeting of The Partnership may be held without all partners in attendance if the partner(s) unable to attend provide in writing his/her approval of the meeting.

FINANCIAL

Tax Classification - The members intend for The Partnership to be taxed as a partnership.

Accounting - The Partnership shall have a tax year beginning January 1 and ending December 31 of each year. Accordingly, The Partnership shall be known as a "calendar year taxpayer." The books of The Partnership shall be maintained on a cash basis with income being recognized when it is received, and expenses recognized when they are paid.

Tax Matters Partner - The Partnership shall appoint a representative to handle tax and accounting matters. _____ shall be appointed to be the tax matters partner.

Banking - The Partnership shall establish bank account(s) with a bank that meets the approval of all partners. At lease two partners will be required to sign checks or withdraw monies from the account(s). No partner shall have the authority to borrow money or obtain lines of credit without express written approval of all partners. This does not, however, apply to credit accounts opened with suppliers. Credit may be obtained from suppliers in the due course of operating the business. Bank statements shall be available to all members with one day's notice, upon their request either verbally or in witting.

Property - Title to all property purchased or leased for The Partnership shall be titled in the name of The Partnership. Partners are hereby granted authority lease equipment on behalf of The Partnership in the due course of business.

OWNERSHIP

New Partners - A new partner may be admitted to The Partnership upon unanimous written agreement of all partners. The addition of a new partner shall not terminate the business of the partnership as the business of The Partnership will simply continue with the new partner on board. The incoming partner will assume his/her portion of the debts, taxes and other liabilities of the partnership as of the date of admittance. The incoming partner may be required to make a cash contribution to The Partnership as determined by the current partners.

Transfers- A member may not transfer, sell, assign, offer as collateral, or pledge his/her interest in The Partnership without prior written approval of the other members.

Sale of Partnership Interest - If a partner leaves the partnership, or is unable to fulfil his or her duties to The Partnership for any reason including death or incapacitation, he/she or his/her estate must sell his/her partnership interest to the remaining partners.

If a partner receives a legitimate offer to purchase his/her partnership interest from an outside buyer, the other partner(s) shall have the right of first refusal to but the selling partner's interest with the same terms and conditions made by the outside buyer. The remaining partners may have 60 days to consider the offer. If the remaining partner(s) do not wish to purchase the selling partner's interest, then the selling partner may then sell to the outside buyer.

Valuation - For the purpose of the sale of a partnership interest, the value of an interest in the partnership shall be the greater of the net worth of the partnership or the value given by an independent appraiser. The costs of valuation of a partnership interest shall be shared by The Partnership and the selling partner.

Dissolution - Upon death or any other event that prevents a partner from participating in the operation of The Partnership, the partnership shall not be dissolved, but continue with the remaining partners.

OTHER PROVISIONS

Authority - Officers of The Partnership and or any member of The Partnership has authority to transact any business or enter into any transaction or carry out any act to complete the formation of the Partnership or further its financial interest in the due course of business with one exception: No member has authority to obtain loans, lines of credit or commit The Partnership to any bank or lending institution without prior written approval of all members.

Disputes - In the event of a dispute between the members regarding this operating agreement or any matter regarding The Partnership, the dispute shall be settled by arbitration according to the rules of the American Arbitration Association. The arbitration service hearing the dispute shall be agreed upon by the members before proceeding. The cost of the arbitration/mediation shall be borne by The Partnership.

If the dispute cannot be settled by arbitration, the matter may go to before a court with jurisdiction in such matters. If the matter goes before a court, then the members individually shall bear the cost of the proceedings. The prevailing party may seek reimbursement of expenses related to the proceedings.

Changes - This document is the only agreement between the members of The Partnership and replaces any verbal or written agreement between members. It cannot be replaced, amended or altered in any way without the approval of the members of The Partnership that adopted and approved the agreement being replaced or amended. If any provision of this agreement is determined to be legally unenforceable, then that provision only shall be stricken from the agreement, leaving the remainder of the agreement in force.

As evidenced by their signatures below, the members hereby adopt this agreement in its entirety and agree to bound by its terms. The signatures do not need to be notarized.

Date

Date	Name	Signature
Date	Name	Signature
Date	Name	Signature
Date	Name	Signature
Date	Name	Signature
Date	Name	Signature

After You've Organized Your Company

Organizing your business is really only the first step of starting a business. After a business is legally organized, there's a list of things you'll need to do before opening for business. I like to look at it like this, incorporating, organizing a limited liability company, or forming a partnership is like having a baby. Your articles of incorporation, articles of incorporation or partnership agreement is like a birth certificate for your business. And, just as if you had a baby, there are a few things you'll need to do next, like getting him/her a Social Security number, and opening a bank account for all that money the grandparents gave the little bundle of joy. The following is a discussion of the more important things you'll need to do after you've organized your business.

If you've never started a business before, you may want to take a look at the "Starting and Operating a Business Series. There's one for each state, and they cover everything you need to know about starting a new business in a particular state. They cover things like permits, licenses, business taxes, insurance, employees, payroll and unemployment taxes, workers comp. and more. For more information, check the order form at the back of the book.

Getting a Federal Tax ID Number

Basically, a Federal Tax ID number is a Social Security number for your business. (It's also called a Employer ID Number.) The IRS uses a Tax ID number to keep up with your business, and maintain a record of the various tax reports and returns that you are required to file, as well as your tax payments. Plus, your bank will require one for opening a checking account. To get a federal tax ID number, you'll need to complete the IRS form number SS-4 included in this section and send or fax it to the IRS office that is listed on pages two and three of the instructions to the form. Your assigned number will arrive by mail.

Since the bank will need a tax ID number to open your business checking account, you'll probably need your tax ID number faster than the IRS can provide it by mail. To get your Tax ID number in a hurry, see page two of the instructions.

Answers to common questions - The date of your incorporation is found on the information you receive from the state after incorporating. The other requested dates will be your best estimates. The name of applicant (Line 1.) is the legal corporate name, LLC name, or partnership name.

A New Business Checklist

Your business name...
If you plan on operating your business under a name that is different from the legal name of the business, you'll need to register the name with the secretary of state or county clerk in which the business operates. Operating your business under a different name is known as operating under a fictitious or assumed name. It is also known as a DBA or "doing business as."

Taxes...
You can guess that there are plenty of local, State and Federal agencies that want taxes from your business. You'll need to get in touch with these folks to let them know you're a new taxpaying entity.

You'll need to get in touch with your state department of revenue or taxation to let them know your business is a new taxpayer. Have then send you any information they have outlining their requirements for new businesses.

Filing your SS-4 will notify the Federal government. You should also call them to get the free information that they offer. They have a booklet called "Taxpayers Starting a Business" that everyone should have. Their telephone number is 1.800.829.1040 or 1.800.829.FORM.

Getting a business permit in the city or the county will put you on their tax rolls. You won't have to notify them. Most telephone books have a government section that lists local, State, and Federal telephone numbers. In most telephone directories, it is the blue pages in the middle of the book.

Permits...

There can be many licenses or permits you'll need depending on the type of business you're in. You'll at least need a county business permit, and a city permit if you're in the city. Some states have state business permits, but they're usually for out of state businesses. There are also Federal permits if you engage in any sort of Federally regulated business like alcohol, tobacco, firearms drug or food manufacturing.

Insurance...

Incorporating or forming an LLC is good protection against lawsuits, but is no replacement for insurance. There are all types of insurance for businesses, but they usually come in a package called "General Business Insurance" or a "Business Policy." It can cover everything from product liability to company vehicles. If you have several employees, you'll need to get workers compensation insurance to cover potential on the job injuries. Your insurance agent can help you get the right coverage for your business.

Accounting...

Keeping the books is a new and sometimes difficult chore for many small business owners. If you turn the job over to a bookkeeper or CPA, expect to pay a monthly fee based on the number of checks that you write. For this fee you can expect to have your books posted and your checkbook balanced. You can also get your quarterly and annual tax returns prepared for an extra fee based on the amount of time it takes to prepare the returns.

If you plan to do your own accounting, you'll save money but doing it yourself will take time away from making money. Accounting isn't hard. It just takes a little getting used to. If you're new at accounting, you may want to take a look at the book "Business Owners Guide to Accounting and Bookkeeping" listed in the brochure in the back of the book.

Keeping your books on the computer will make your life a lot easier because the computer will even prepare some or all you your tax returns. There are many software packages available, and I've tried them all. I like Quick Books the best.

Employees...

If you have employees other than yourself, you'll need consider all the State and Federal regulations regarding employees. The books entitled "Legal Guide for Starting and Running a Small Business" and the "Starting and Operating a Business Series" are excellent sources of information in this area.

Free help...

Volumes can, and have been written about the subjects in this chapter. If you desire additional information on any of these subjects, or how to start a business in general, there are several excellent places to get free or low cost information about starting a business. Here's a list of the best:

- *The U.S. Small Business Administration sponsors small business development centers (SBDCs) at community colleges in your area. These SBDCs offer free consulting to small business owners. These offices are staffed by experienced business people and can provide invaluable help to you. To find one in your area, call the community colleges in your area and ask them if they have a small business development center on campus. If you have no luck, call your local chamber of commerce and ask them. Take advantage of this program funded by your tax dollars.*

- *The U.S. Small Business Administration also sponsors SCORE offices in your area. Separate from the SBDCs, these centers are staffed by retired executives in your area, and also provide free consulting. To find SCORE offices in your area, look in your telephone directory under the Federal Government listings under Small Business Administration SCORE office.*

- *The SBA publishes books, videos, and pamphlets at little or no cost to you. For a list of these publications, write SBA Publications, P.O. Box 30, Denver CO 80201-0030, and request a catalog.*

- *Your chamber of commerce is there to help local businesses. They are familiar with the requirements of local and state governments and can provide you with invaluable information that will save you a lot of time and mistakes. Call them and ask if they have any information about starting a new business.*

Form **SS-4**
(Rev. December 1995)
Department of the Treasury
Internal Revenue Service

Application for Employer Identification Number

(For use by employers, corporations, partnerships, trusts, estates, churches, government agencies, certain individuals, and others. See instructions.)

▶ **Keep a copy for your records.**

EIN

OMB No. 1545-0003

Please type or print clearly.

1 Name of applicant (Legal name) (See instructions.)

2 Trade name of business (if different from name on line 1)

3 Executor, trustee, "care of" name

4a Mailing address (street address) (room, apt., or suite no.)

5a Business address (if different from address on lines 4a and 4b)

4b City, state, and ZIP code

5b City, state, and ZIP code

6 County and state where principal business is located

7 Name of principal officer, general partner, grantor, owner, or trustor—SSN required (See instructions.) ▶

8a Type of entity (Check only one box.) (See instructions.)
- ☐ Sole proprietor (SSN) _____
- ☐ Partnership
- ☐ REMIC
- ☐ State/local government
- ☐ Other nonprofit organization (specify) ▶ _____
- ☐ Other (specify) ▶
- ☐ Personal service corp.
- ☐ Limited liability co.
- ☐ National Guard
- ☐ Estate (SSN of decedent) _____
- ☐ Plan administrator-SSN _____
- ☐ Other corporation (specify) ▶ _____
- ☐ Trust
- ☐ Federal Government/military
- ☐ Farmers' cooperative
- ☐ Church or church-controlled organization

(enter GEN if applicable) _____

8b If a corporation, name the state or foreign country (if applicable) where incorporated

State

Foreign country

9 Reason for applying (Check only one box.)
- ☐ Started new business (specify) ▶ _____
- ☐ Hired employees
- ☐ Created a pension plan (specify type) ▶
- ☐ Banking purpose (specify) ▶ _____
- ☐ Changed type of organization (specify) ▶ _____
- ☐ Purchased going business
- ☐ Created a trust (specify) ▶ _____
- ☐ Other (specify) ▶

10 Date business started or acquired (Mo., day, year) (See instructions.)

11 Closing month of accounting year (See instructions.)

12 First date wages or annuities were paid or will be paid (Mo., day, year). **Note:** *If applicant is a withholding agent, enter date income will first be paid to nonresident alien. (Mo., day, year)* . . . . ▶

13 Highest number of employees expected in the next 12 months. **Note:** *If the applicant does not expect to have any employees during the period, enter -0-. (See instructions.)* . . . ▶

Nonagricultural	Agricultural	Household

14 Principal activity (See instructions.) ▶

15 Is the principal business activity manufacturing? . . . . ☐ **Yes** ☐ **No**
If "Yes," principal product and raw material used ▶

16 To whom are most of the products or services sold? Please check the appropriate box. ☐ Business (wholesale)
☐ Public (retail) ☐ Other (specify) ▶ ☐ N/A

17a Has the applicant ever applied for an identification number for this or any other business? . . . . ☐ **Yes** ☐ **No**
Note: *If "Yes," please complete lines 17b and 17c.*

17b If you checked "Yes" on line 17a, give applicant's legal name and trade name shown on prior application, if different from line 1 or 2 above.
Legal name ▶   Trade name ▶

17c Approximate date when and city and state where the application was filed. Enter previous employer identification number if known.
Approximate date when filed (Mo., day, year) | City and state where filed | Previous EIN

Under penalties of perjury, I declare that I have examined this application, and to the best of my knowledge and belief, it is true, correct, and complete.

Business telephone number (include area code)

Fax telephone number (include area code)

Name and title (Please type or print clearly.) ▶

Signature ▶   Date ▶

Note: *Do not write below this line. For official use only.*

Please leave blank ▶	Geo.	Ind.	Class	Size	Reason for applying

For Paperwork Reduction Act Notice, see page 4.   Cat. No. 16055N   Form **SS-4** (Rev. 12-95)

General Instructions

Section references are to the Internal Revenue Code unless otherwise noted.

Purpose of Form

Use Form SS-4 to apply for an employer identification number (EIN). An EIN is a nine-digit number (for example, 12-3456789) assigned to sole proprietors, corporations, partnerships, estates, trusts, and other entities for filing and reporting purposes. The information you provide on this form will establish your filing and reporting requirements.

Who Must File

You must file this form if you have not obtained an EIN before and:

● You pay wages to one or more employees including household employees.

● You are required to have an EIN to use on any return, statement, or other document, even if you are not an employer.

● You are a withholding agent required to withhold taxes on income, other than wages, paid to a nonresident alien (individual, corporation, partnership, etc.). A withholding agent may be an agent, broker, fiduciary, manager, tenant, or spouse, and is required to file **Form 1042,** Annual Withholding Tax Return for U.S. Source Income of Foreign Persons.

● You file **Schedule C,** Profit or Loss From Business, or **Schedule F,** Profit or Loss From Farming, of **Form 1040,** U.S. Individual Income Tax Return, **and** have a Keogh plan or are required to file excise, employment, information, or alcohol, tobacco, or firearms returns.

The following must use EINs even if they do not have any employees:

● State and local agencies who serve as tax reporting agents for public assistance recipients, under Rev. Proc. 80-4, 1980-1 C.B. 581, should obtain a separate EIN for this reporting. See **Household employer** on page 3.

● Trusts, except the following:

1. Certain grantor-owned revocable trusts. (See the **Instructions for Form 1041.**)

2. Individual Retirement Arrangement (IRA) trusts, unless the trust has to file **Form 990-T,** Exempt Organization Business Income Tax Return. (See the **Instructions for Form 990-T.**)

3. Certain trusts that are considered household employers can use the trust EIN to report and pay the social security and Medicare taxes, Federal unemployment tax (FUTA) and withheld Federal income tax. A separate EIN is not necessary.

● Estates

● Partnerships

● REMICs (real estate mortgage investment conduits) (See the **Instructions for Form 1066,** U.S. Real Estate Mortgage Investment Conduit Income Tax Return.)

● Corporations

● Nonprofit organizations (churches, clubs, etc.)

● Farmers' cooperatives

● Plan administrators (A plan administrator is the person or group of persons specified as the administrator by the instrument under which the plan is operated.)

When To Apply for a New EIN

New Business.—If you become the new owner of an existing business, **do not** use the EIN of the former owner. IF YOU ALREADY HAVE AN EIN, USE THAT NUMBER. If you do not have an EIN, apply for one on this form. If you become the "owner" of a corporation by acquiring its stock, use the corporation's EIN.

Changes in Organization or Ownership.—If you already have an EIN, you may need to get a new one if either the organization or ownership of your business changes. If you incorporate a sole proprietorship or form a partnership, you must get a new EIN. However, **do not** apply for a new EIN if you change only the name of your business.

Note: *If you are electing to be an "S corporation," be sure you file* **Form 2553,** *Election by a Small Business Corporation.*

File Only One Form SS-4.—File only one Form SS-4, regardless of the number of businesses operated or trade names under which a business operates. However, each corporation in an affiliated group must file a separate application.

EIN Applied For, But Not Received.—If you do not have an EIN by the time a return is due, write "Applied for" and the date you applied in the space shown for the number. **Do not** show your social security number as an EIN on returns.

If you do not have an EIN by the time a tax deposit is due, send your payment to the Internal Revenue Service Center for your filing area. (See **Where To Apply** below.) Make your check or money order payable to Internal Revenue Service and show your name (as shown on Form SS-4), address, type of tax, period covered, and date you applied for an EIN. Send an explanation with the deposit.

For more information about EINs, see **Pub. 583,** Starting a Business and Keeping Records, and **Pub. 1635,** Understanding Your EIN.

How To Apply

You can apply for an EIN either by mail or by telephone. You can get an EIN immediately by calling the Tele-TIN phone number for the service center for your state, or you can send the completed Form SS-4 directly to the service center to receive your EIN in the mail.

Application by Tele-TIN.—Under the Tele-TIN program, you can receive your EIN over the telephone and use it immediately to file a return or make a payment. To receive an EIN by phone, complete Form SS-4, then call the Tele-TIN phone number listed for your state under **Where To Apply.** The person making the call must be authorized to sign the form. (See **Signature block** on page 4.)

An IRS representative will use the information from the Form SS-4 to establish your account and assign you an EIN. Write the number you are given on the upper right-hand corner of the form, sign and date it.

Mail or FAX the signed SS-4 **within 24 hours** *to the Tele-TIN Unit at the service center address for your state. The IRS representative will give you the FAX number. The FAX numbers are also listed in Pub. 1635.*

Taxpayer representatives can receive their client's EIN by phone if they first send a facsimile (FAX) of a completed **Form 2848,** Power of Attorney and Declaration of Representative, or **Form 8821,** Tax Information Authorization, to the Tele-TIN unit. The Form 2848 or Form 8821 will be used solely to release the EIN to the representative authorized on the form.

Application by Mail.—Complete Form SS-4 at least 4 to 5 weeks before you will need an EIN. Sign and date the application and mail it to the service center address for your state. You will receive your EIN in the mail in approximately 4 weeks.

Where To Apply

The Tele-TIN phone numbers listed below will involve a long-distance charge to callers outside of the local calling area and can be used only to apply for an EIN. THE NUMBERS MAY CHANGE WITHOUT NOTICE. Use 1-800-829-1040 to verify a number or to ask about an application by mail or other Federal tax matters.

If your principal business, office or agency, or legal residence in the case of an individual, is located in:	Call the Tele-TIN phone number shown or file with the Internal Revenue Service Center at:
Florida, Georgia, South Carolina	Attn: Entity Control Atlanta, GA 39901 (404) 455-2360
New Jersey, New York City and counties of Nassau, Rockland, Suffolk, and Westchester	Attn: Entity Control Holtsville, NY 00501 (516) 447-4955
New York (all other counties), Connecticut, Maine, Massachusetts, New Hampshire, Rhode Island, Vermont	Attn: Entity Control Andover, MA 05501 (508) 474-9717
Illinois, Iowa, Minnesota, Missouri, Wisconsin	Attn: Entity Control Stop 57A 2306 E. Bannister Rd. Kansas City, MO 64131 (816) 926-5999
Delaware, District of Columbia, Maryland, Pennsylvania, Virginia	Attn: Entity Control Philadelphia, PA 19255 (215) 574-2400
Indiana, Kentucky, Michigan, Ohio, West Virginia	Attn: Entity Control Cincinnati, OH 45999 (606) 292-5467
Kansas, New Mexico, Oklahoma, Texas	Attn: Entity Control Austin, TX 73301 (512) 460-7843

Alaska, Arizona, California (counties of Alpine, Amador, Butte, Calaveras, Colusa, Contra Costa, Del Norte, El Dorado, Glenn, Humboldt, Lake, Lassen, Marin, Mendocino, Modoc, Napa, Nevada, Placer, Plumas, Sacramento, San Joaquin, Shasta, Sierra, Siskiyou, Solano, Sonoma, Sutter, Tehama, Trinity, Yolo, and Yuba), Colorado, Idaho, Montana, Nebraska, Nevada, North Dakota, Oregon, South Dakota, Utah, Washington, Wyoming	Attn: Entity Control Mail Stop 6271-T P.O. Box 9950 Ogden, UT 84409 (801) 620-7645
California (all other counties), Hawaii	Attn: Entity Control Fresno, CA 93888 (209) 452-4010
Alabama, Arkansas, Louisiana, Mississippi, North Carolina, Tennessee	Attn: Entity Control Memphis, TN 37501 (901) 365-5970

If you have no legal residence, principal place of business, or principal office or agency in any state, file your form with the Internal Revenue Service Center, Philadelphia, PA 19255 or call 215-574-2400.

Specific Instructions

The instructions that follow are for those items that are not self-explanatory. Enter N/A (nonapplicable) on the lines that do not apply.

Line 1.—Enter the legal name of the entity applying for the EIN exactly as it appears on the social security card, charter, or other applicable legal document.

Individuals.—Enter the first name, middle initial, and last name. If you are a sole proprietor, enter your individual name, not your business name. Do not use abbreviations or nicknames.

Trusts.—Enter the name of the trust.

Estate of a decedent.—Enter the name of the estate.

Partnerships.—Enter the legal name of the partnership as it appears in the partnership agreement. **Do not** list the names of the partners on line 1. See the specific instructions for line 7.

Corporations.—Enter the corporate name as it appears in the corporation charter or other legal document creating it.

Plan administrators.—Enter the name of the plan administrator. A plan administrator who already has an EIN should use that number.

Line 2.—Enter the trade name of the business if different from the legal name. The trade name is the "doing business as" name.

Note: *Use the full legal name on line 1 on all tax returns filed for the entity. However, if you enter a trade name on line 2 and choose to use the trade name instead of the legal name, enter the trade name on all returns you file. To prevent processing delays and errors, **always** use either the legal name only or the trade name only on all tax returns.*

Line 3.—Trusts enter the name of the trustee. Estates enter the name of the executor, administrator, or other fiduciary. If the entity applying has a designated person to receive tax information, enter that person's name as the "care of"

person. Print or type the first name, middle initial, and last name.

Line 7.—Enter the first name, middle initial, last name, and social security number (SSN) of a principal officer if the business is a corporation; of a general partner if a partnership; or of a grantor, owner, or trustor if a trust.

Line 8a.—Check the box that best describes the type of entity applying for the EIN. If not specifically mentioned, check the "Other" box and enter the type of entity. Do not enter N/A.

Sole proprietor.—Check this box if you file Schedule C or F (Form 1040) and have a Keogh plan, or are required to file excise, employment, information, or alcohol, tobacco, or firearms returns. Enter your SSN in the space provided.

REMIC.—Check this box if the entity has elected to be treated as a real estate mortgage investment conduit (REMIC). See the **Instructions for Form 1066** for more information.

Other nonprofit organization.—Check this box if the nonprofit organization is other than a church or church-controlled organization and specify the type of nonprofit organization (for example, an educational organization).

If the organization also seeks tax-exempt status, you must file either **Package 1023** or **Package 1024,** Application for Recognition of Exemption. Get **Pub. 557,** Tax-Exempt Status for Your Organization, for more information.

Group exemption number (GEN).—If the organization is covered by a group exemption letter, enter the four-digit GEN. (Do not confuse the GEN with the nine-digit EIN.) If you do not know the GEN, contact the parent organization. Get Pub. 557 for more information about group exemption numbers.

Withholding agent.—If you are a withholding agent required to file Form 1042, check the "Other" box and enter "Withholding agent."

Personal service corporation.—Check this box if the entity is a personal service corporation. An entity is a personal service corporation for a tax year only if:

● The principal activity of the entity during the testing period (prior tax year) for the tax year is the performance of personal services substantially by employee-owners, and

● The employee-owners own 10% of the fair market value of the outstanding stock in the entity on the last day of the testing period.

Personal services include performance of services in such fields as health, law, accounting, or consulting. For more information about personal service corporations, see the **Instructions for Form 1120,** U.S. Corporation Income Tax Return, and **Pub. 542,** Tax Information on Corporations.

Limited liability co.—See the definition of limited liability company in the **Instructions for Form 1065.** If you are classified as a partnership for Federal income tax

purposes, mark the "Limited liability co." checkbox. If you are classified as a corporation for Federal income tax purposes, mark the "Other corporation" checkbox and write "Limited liability co." in the space provided.

Plan administrator.—If the plan administrator is an individual, enter the plan administrator's SSN in the space provided.

Other corporation.—This box is for any corporation other than a personal service corporation. If you check this box, enter the type of corporation (such as insurance company) in the space provided.

Household employer.—If you are an individual, check the "Other" box and enter "Household employer" and your SSN. If you are a state or local agency serving as a tax reporting agent for public assistance recipients who become household employers, check the "Other" box and enter "Household employer agent." If you are a trust that qualifies as a household employer, you do not need a separate EIN for reporting tax information relating to household employees; use the EIN of the trust.

Line 9.—Check only **one** box. Do not enter N/A.

Started new business.—Check this box if you are starting a new business that requires an EIN. If you check this box, enter the type of business being started. **Do not** apply if you already have an EIN and are only adding another place of business.

Hired employees.—Check this box if the existing business is requesting an EIN because it has hired or is hiring employees and is therefore required to file employment tax returns. **Do not** apply if you already have an EIN and are only hiring employees. For information on the applicable employment taxes for family members, see **Circular E,** Employer's Tax Guide (Publication 15).

Created a pension plan.—Check this box if you have created a pension plan and need this number for reporting purposes. Also, enter the type of plan created.

Banking purpose.—Check this box if you are requesting an EIN for banking purposes only, and enter the banking purpose (for example, a bowling league for depositing dues or an investment club for dividend and interest reporting).

Changed type of organization.—Check this box if the business is changing its type of organization, for example, if the business was a sole proprietorship and has been incorporated or has become a partnership. If you check this box, specify in the space provided the type of change made, for example, "from sole proprietorship to partnership."

Purchased going business.—Check this box if you purchased an existing business. **Do not** use the former owner's EIN. **Do not** apply for a new EIN if you already have one. Use your own EIN.

Created a trust.—Check this box if you created a trust, and enter the type of trust created.

Note: *Do not file this form if you are the grantor/owner of certain revocable trusts. You must use your SSN for the trust. See the Instructions for Form 1041.*

Other (specify).—Check this box if you are requesting an EIN for any reason other than those for which there are checkboxes, and enter the reason.

Line 10.—If you are starting a new business, enter the starting date of the business. If the business you acquired is already operating, enter the date you acquired the business. Trusts should enter the date the trust was legally created. Estates should enter the date of death of the decedent whose name appears on line 1 or the date when the estate was legally funded.

Line 11.—Enter the last month of your accounting year or tax year. An accounting or tax year is usually 12 consecutive months, either a calendar year or a fiscal year (including a period of 52 or 53 weeks). A calendar year is 12 consecutive months ending on December 31. A fiscal year is either 12 consecutive months ending on the last day of any month other than December or a 52-53 week year. For more information on accounting periods, see **Pub. 538,** Accounting Periods and Methods.

Individuals.—Your tax year generally will be a calendar year.

Partnerships.—Partnerships generally must adopt the tax year of either (a) the majority partners; (b) the principal partners; (c) the tax year that results in the least aggregate (total) deferral of income; or (d) some other tax year. (See the **Instructions for Form 1065,** U.S. Partnership Return of Income, for more information.)

REMIC.—REMICs must have a calendar year as their tax year.

Personal service corporations.—A personal service corporation generally must adopt a calendar year unless:

● It can establish a business purpose for having a different tax year, or

● It elects under section 444 to have a tax year other than a calendar year.

Trusts.—Generally, a trust must adopt a calendar year except for the following:

● Tax-exempt trusts,

● Charitable trusts, and

● Grantor-owned trusts.

Line 12.—If the business has or will have employees, enter the date on which the business began or will begin to pay wages. If the business does not plan to have employees, enter N/A.

Withholding agent.—Enter the date you began or will begin to pay income to a nonresident alien. This also applies to individuals who are required to file Form 1042 to report alimony paid to a nonresident alien.

Line 13.—For a definition of agricultural labor (farmworker), see **Circular A,** Agricultural Employer's Tax Guide (Publication 51).

Line 14.—Generally, enter the exact type of business being operated (for example, advertising agency, farm, food or beverage establishment, labor union, real estate agency, steam laundry, rental of coin-operated vending machine, or investment club). Also state if the business will involve the sale or distribution of alcoholic beverages.

Governmental.—Enter the type of organization (state, county, school district, municipality, etc.).

Nonprofit organization (other than governmental).—Enter whether organized for religious, educational, or humane purposes, and the principal activity (for example, religious organization—hospital, charitable).

Mining and quarrying.—Specify the process and the principal product (for example, mining bituminous coal, contract drilling for oil, or quarrying dimension stone).

Contract construction.—Specify whether general contracting or special trade contracting. Also, show the type of work normally performed (for example, general contractor for residential buildings or electrical subcontractor).

Food or beverage establishments.—Specify the type of establishment and state whether you employ workers who receive tips (for example, lounge—yes).

Trade.—Specify the type of sales and the principal line of goods sold (for example, wholesale dairy products, manufacturer's representative for mining machinery, or retail hardware).

Manufacturing.—Specify the type of establishment operated (for example, sawmill or vegetable cannery).

Signature block.—The application must be signed by (a) the individual, if the applicant is an individual, (b) the president, vice president, or other principal officer, if the applicant is a corporation, (c) a responsible and duly authorized member or officer having knowledge of its affairs, if the applicant is a partnership or other unincorporated organization, or (d) the fiduciary, if the applicant is a trust or estate.

Some Useful Publications

You may get the following publications for additional information on the subjects covered on this form. To get these and other free forms and publications, call 1-800-TAX-FORM (1-800-829-3676). You should receive your order or notification of its status within 7 to 15 workdays of your call.

Use your computer.—If you subscribe to an on-line service, ask if IRS information is available and, if so, how to access it. You can also get information through IRIS, the Internal Revenue Information Services, on FedWorld, a government bulletin board. Tax forms, instructions, publications, and other IRS information, are available through IRIS.

IRIS is accessible directly by calling 703-321-8020. On the Internet, you can telnet to fedworld.gov. or, for file transfer protocol services, connect to ftp.fedworld.gov. If you are using the WorldWide Web, connect to http://www.ustreas.gov

FedWorld's help desk offers technical assistance on accessing IRIS (not tax help) during regular business hours at 703-487-4608. The IRIS menus offer information on available file formats and software needed to read and print files. You must print the forms to use them; the forms are not designed to be filled out on-screen.

Tax forms, instructions, and publications are also available on CD-ROM, including prior-year forms starting with the 1991 tax year. For ordering information and software requirements, contact the Government Printing Office's Superintendent of Documents (202-512-1800) or Federal Bulletin Board (202-512-1387).

Pub. 1635, Understanding Your EIN

Pub. 15, Employer's Tax Guide

Pub. 15-A, Employer's Supplemental Tax Guide

Pub. 538, Accounting Periods and Methods

Pub. 541, Tax Information on Partnerships

Pub. 542, Tax Information on Corporations

Pub. 557, Tax-Exempt Status for Your Organization

Pub. 583, Starting a Business and Keeping Records

Package 1023, Application for Recognition of Exemption

Package 1024, Application for Recognition of Exemption Under Section 501(a) or for Determination Under Section 120

Paperwork Reduction Act Notice

We ask for the information on this form to carry out the Internal Revenue laws of the United States. You are required to give us the information. We need it to ensure that you are complying with these laws and to allow us to figure and collect the right amount of tax.

The time needed to complete and file this form will vary depending on individual circumstances. The estimated average time is:

Recordkeeping . . . . 7 min.

Learning about the law or the form . . . . . . 18 min.

Preparing the form . . . . . 45 min.

Copying, assembling, and sending the form to the IRS . . 20 min.

If you have comments concerning the accuracy of these time estimates or suggestions for making this form simpler, we would be happy to hear from you. You can write to the Tax Forms Committee, Western Area Distribution Center, Rancho Cordova, CA 95743-0001. **Do not** send this form to this address. Instead, see **Where To Apply** on page 2.

 Printed on recycled paper

Chapter 6

QuickStart Forms and Instructions

Whether you read the entire book, or came straight here after reading chapter one–*Welcome!* This is the QuickStart chapter. Here you'll find simplified instructions for organizing your corporation, limited liability company, or partnership. Accordingly, it is divided into three parts.

Although you should read the chapter that explains in detail how to form the type of business that you want, you can organize your business with the instructions in this chapter. These are the same step-by-step instructions that you'll find in chapters two, three, and four–they're just condensed so you can get done faster. If you need additional instructions or clarification on a particular step, refer to the given page reference in the book. Also in this chapter, you'll find the forms you'll need to file with the state. *Now let's get to work...*

PART ONE - FORMING A CORPORATION

Forming a corporation in Indiana is easy. The centerpiece of the entire process is the "Articles of Incorporation." Filing this document with the state brings your corporation to life and starts the process of organizing your business. The Articles of Incorporation required by Indiana law is a basic form that contains information about the corporation, the stock it issues, its appointed representative, and its organizer. It is filed with a state agency, the Corporations Division of the Indiana Secretary of State's office. Their telephone number is (317) 232-6576, and their office hours are 8-5:30 Monday-Friday.

After you've filed the Articles of Incorporation with the state and received proof of the filing from them, you'll need to attend to some other organizational matters like naming your officers and directors, issuing stock, and setting up your corporate records. When you've done all of this, the incorporating process is complete. After incorporating, you'll need to get a business permit and attend to some other new business formalities discussed in Chapter Five. Only one person is required to form a corporation in Indiana.

Here are the basic steps for forming a corporation:

Step 1.   *Choose a corporate name.*
Step 2.   *File your paperwork.*
Step 3.   *Take care of organizational matters.*
Step 4.   *Prepare a corporate record book.*

Below, you'll find each of these steps discussed in detail. The check boxes under each step list the action(s) you'll need to take, and the paragraphs that follow tell you how to accomplish them.

Step 1. Choose a Corporate Name

❏ *Choose a corporate name that meets state requirements and includes "Inc."*

❏ *Make sure another company isn't already using the name.*

Choosing a name for your corporation is always fun. Your corporate name can be descriptive of your business or not. The name "Dean's Bookstore, Inc." gives everyone a pretty good idea of what the corporation's business is, and "Nortrex Corporation" does not. Whatever you name your corporation, the name must meet a few requirements outlined by state law, and of course, you'll want to make sure someone else isn't already using the name.

State requirements...
Specifically, the corporate name must contain either Corporation, Incorporated, Limited, Company, or an abbreviation of one of these words, Corp., Inc., Ltd., or Co. Choose whichever looks or sounds best with the name. Most people use "Inc."

In general, the name may not include the words bank, trust, trustee, insurance or any similar word without satisfying banking or insurance regulations. It may not imply that the corporation is authorized to transact any business for which it has not been approved, or imply affiliation with any other organization or the Federal government unless it is authorized to do so. Also, if you are a doctor, architect, or belong to a similarly licensed profession, you may need to form a professional corporation and provide proof that you are licensed to operate a business in your field.

The corporate name may not be the same or deceptively similar to any other name registered with the Secretary of State. Changing the corporate identifier will not change the name - Jones Inc., and Jones Corporation is the same name. Also, the name may not be misleading to the public.

Name availability...
Before filing your Articles, you'll want to make sure that another business registered with the State is already using "your" name. To do this, simply call the Corporation Division at (312) 232-6576. When the representative answers, tell him/her you'd like to check the availability of a name. See page 89 for a role play of a typical conversation.

Not only should your name differ from those on file with the State, you'll want to make sure that another business in your geographic area isn't using it. This includes incorporated and non-incorporated businesses. Checking the availability of a corporate name with the State only checks for business names registered with them. An unincorporated business, like a partnership or sole proprietorship that is not listed on their computer, could already be using "your" name. A quick check through the telephone book will help determine this.

Also, if you're going regional or nationwide, you may consider protecting the name by registering it as a trademark with the state and/or the Patent and Trademark office in Washington, DC. The first business using a name in a geographic area has the exclusive right to use the name. If a name is registered Federally, the geographic area includes the entire country. See the brochure at the back of this book for a step-by-step guide on the subject of trademarks.

Fictitious or assumed names...
Incorporating under one name and conducting business under another is known as using a "fictitious" or "assumed" name, or "doing business as" (dba). Using a fictitious or assumed name allows you to form your corporation using a "generic" name, and transact business under one or more descriptive names. For example, the company "Brown, Inc." could use a fictitious name and transact business as "Consumer Publishing Corp."

To use a fictitious name, you'll need to file a "Certificate of Assumed Business Name" with the County Recorder for your county and the Secretary of State. (You'll do this only *after* the Articles of Incorporation are filed.) File the document with the county first, then file it with the State. (It must have the county's stamp on it before it can be filed with the State.) The form is available from the Corporation Division at (312) 232-6576. The county filing fee varies by county. The State filing fee is $30.

If you need more information regarding this step, see page 27.

Step 2. File Your Paperwork

❑ *Complete the Articles of Incorporation form included in this chapter.*

❑ *Send or take the Articles and one copy to the Corporation Division's office. Include a check for $90.*

Filing your Articles of Incorporation with the state begins your corporate existence. To file your Articles, simply complete and sign the "Articles of Incorporation" form included in this chapter, and send or take it with the filing fee to the Secretary of State's office. The instructions and address are on the back of the form. The State requests that the Articles be typewritten. A computer disk that contains the forms in this book is available from Consumer Publishing by calling 1-800-677-2462.

Depending on the State's work load, it will take from 1-4 weeks to have your articles filed. As verification of your incorporation, a receipt for the filing will be returned to you.

If you're in a hurry, you can get faster service if you overnight or deliver the Articles yourself. Overnighted or hand-delivered filings are returned in 24-48 hours. If you send the Articles via an overnight service like FedEx, be sure to include a prepaid airbill so the Corporation Division can send the filed copy back to you.

Payment of the fees can be made by personal or business check, or a money order made payable to the "Indiana Secretary of State."

If you need more information regarding this step, see page 40.

Step 3. Take Care of Organizational Matters

❑ *Choose your officers and directors.*

❑ *When proof of filing returns from the State, complete the form "Minutes of Organizational Meeting" on page 65. Keep it with your corporate records.*

❑ *Issue stock certificates to each shareholder.*

Organizational matters consist of appointing officers and directors, issuing stock and other formalities. They are taken care of at a meeting known as "the organizational meeting." The organizational meeting is held after the Articles of Incorporation has been filed with the state. Most people don't actually hold a meeting, they just take the form on page 65, complete it, and file it in their corporate records book.

Officers and directors...

Officers and directors can be anyone you choose. They don't need to be shareholders of the corporation, but they must be of legal age.

The law requires that your corporation have a president, a secretary, and a treasurer. The law doesn't say that these offices can't be held by the same person.

Stock registration...

If you want to sell stock to investors or others who will not take part in the day-to-day operations of the company, you may need to register your stock with the Securities Division of The Secretary of State's Office. Their telephone number is (317) 232-6681. Transactions are usually exempt from registration with the state if all the following conditions are met. If you have further questions, about stock registration, see page 34.

1. *The number of Indiana residents purchasing the stock in the last 12 months is 20 or fewer, and*
2. *The stock is not offered in sales literature or advertised, and*
3. *Commission is not paid to anyone for selling the stock of the corporation, and*
4. *The shareholders are purchasing the stock as an investment and not for resale.*

If you need more information regarding this step, see page 34.

Step 4. Prepare a Corporate Record Book.

❑ *Prepare or purchase a corporate record book with corporate seal.*

❑ *Place all your documents, filing receipts and minutes in the record book.*

❑ *Use the corporate seal to emboss the stock certificates and Minutes of Organizational Meeting.*

❑ *After you've completed the steps above, take a look at Chapter 5 for a checklist of some things you'll need to do after incorporating.*

Properly maintained records are the only evidence of a correctly formed and legally valid corporation. They are vital in preventing someone from winning a lawsuit against you by "piercing" your corporate veil. Your corporate records are probably the first thing the IRS will ask to see if you ever get audited. Also, bankers and investors will want to see your records if you seek financing for your business.

Most people use a customized corporate "outfit" or "kit" to organize their records. A corporate outfit typically includes an engraved corporate seal, color stock certificates typeset with the corporate name, standard meeting forms and bylaws, all separated by tabbed dividers and enclosed in a nice binder with the corporate name embossed in gold lettering on the spine.

You can get a corporate outfit at most legal stationery stores. If you can't find one locally, they are available from Consumer Publishing at 1-800-677-2462. Our outfits are usually shipped within 24 hours including the engraved corporate seal. The brochure in the back of the book has complete information.

Unless you're sure that your corporate name is available, you should wait until your Articles of Incorporation is processed by the state before ordering a corporate outfit. Only after filing the Articles of Incorporation will you be sure that "your" name is available and okay to use.

You'll need the corporate seal for embossing your stock certificates and for the "Minutes of Organizational Meeting." (In the previous step) Also, most banks require a corporate seal to open a bank account.

If you need more information regarding this step, see page 47.

After completing all four of these steps, be sure to review chapter five for a checklist of things every new business needs to do before commencing business - things like getting a business permit and a Federal tax ID number.

PART TWO - FORMING A LIMITED LIABILITY COMPANY

The process of forming a limited liability company is almost the same as that of forming a corporation. Usually, the only difference is the form that you file with the state and the filing fee.

The centerpiece of the LLC organization process in Indiana is a document known as the "Articles of Organization." Filing this form with the State brings your limited liability company to life and begins the process of organizing your business. The Articles of Organization required by Indiana law is a simple form that contains basic information about your company. It is filed with a state agency, the Corporation Division of the Indiana Secretary of State's office. Their telephone number is (317) 232-6576, and their office hours are 8-5:30 Monday-Friday. Only one member is required to organize an LLC in Indiana.

After you've filed the Articles of Organization and received proof of your filing from the state, you'll need to attend to some other organizational matters like naming your officers and managers, issuing member certificates, and setting up your company records. After the legal organization of your limited liability company is complete, you'll need to get a business permit, and attend to a few other new business formalities outlined in Chapter Five. Here are the basic steps for forming a limited liability company:

Step 1.   Choose a company name.
Step 2.   File your paperwork.
Step 3.   Take care of organizational matters.
Step 4.   Prepare a company record book.

Next, you'll find each of these steps discussed in detail. The check boxes under each step list the action(s) you'll need to take, and the paragraphs that follow tell you how to accomplish them.

Step 1. Choose a Company Name

❑ *Choose a company name that meets state requirements and includes "LLC"*

❑ *Make sure another company isn't already using the name.*

Choosing a name for your company is always fun. Your company name can be descriptive of your business or not. The name "Dean's Bookstore, LLC" gives everyone a pretty good idea of what the company does for a living, and "Nortrex LLC" does not. Whatever you name your company, the name must meet a few requirements outlined by state law, and of course, you'll want to make sure someone else isn't already using the name.

State requirements...

Specifically, the company name must contain either limited liability company, or the abbreviations LLC or L.L.C. Choose whichever looks or sounds best with the name. Most people use "LLC."

In general, the name may not include the words bank, trust, trustee, insurance or any similar word without satisfying banking or insurance regulations. It may not imply that the LLC is authorized to transact any business for which it has not been approved, or imply affiliation with any other organization or the Federal government unless it is authorized to do so. Also, if you are a doctor, architect, or belong to a similarly licenced profession, you might need to form a professional LLC or corporation, and provide proof that you are licensed to operate a business in your field.

The name may not be the same or deceptively similar to any other name registered with the State. Also, the name may not be misleading to the public. Changing the LLC identifier will not change the name - Jones LLC, and Jones Limited Liability Company is the same name.

Name availability...

Before filing your Articles, you'll want to make sure that another business registered with the State is already using "your" name. To do this, simply call the Corporation Division at (317) 232-6576. When the representative answers, tell him/her you'd like to check the availability of a name. See page 89 for a role play of a typical conversation.

Not only should your name differ from those on file with the State, you'll want to make sure that another business in your geographic area isn't using it. This includes LLCs, incorporated and non-incorporated businesses. Checking the availability of a name with the State only checks for business names registered with them. Bear in mind that an unincorporated business, like a partnership or sole proprietorship, that is not listed on their computer, may already be using "your" name. A quick check through the telephone book will help determine this.

Also, if you're going regional or nationwide, you may consider protecting the name by registering it as a trademark with the state and/or the Patent and Trademark office in Washington DC. The first business using a name in a geographic area has the exclusive right to use the name. If a name is registered Federally, the geographic area includes the entire country. A good book on the subject of trademarks is listed in the brochure at the back of this book.

Fictitious or assumed names...

Organizing your LLC under one name and conducting business under another is known as using a "fictitious" or "assumed" name, or "doing business as" (dba). Using a fictitious or assumed name allows you to form your LLC using a "generic" name, and transact business under one or more descriptive names. For example, the company "Brown, LLC ." could use a fictitious name and transact business as "Consumer Publishing LLC."

To use a fictitious name, you'll need to file a "Certificate of Assumed Business Name" with the County Recorder for your county and the Secretary of State. (You'll do this only *after* the Articles of Organization are filed. File the document with the county first, then file it with the Secretary of State. (It must have the county's stamp on it before it can be filed with the state.) The form is available from the Corporation Division at (317) 232-6576. The county filing fee varies by county. The State filing fee is $30.

If you need more information regarding this step, see page 87.

Step 2. File Your Paperwork

❏ *Complete the Articles of Organization form included in this chapter.*

❏ *Take or send it and one copy to the Corporation Division's office. Include a check for $90.*

Filing your Articles of Organization with the state marks the beginning of your LLC's existence. To file your Articles, all you need to do is complete and sign the Articles of Organization form included in this chapter and send or take it and one copy with the filing fee of $90 to the Corporation Division's office. The instructions and address are on the back of the form. The State requests that filings be typewritten. A computer disk with the forms in this book is available from Consumer Publishing by calling 1-800-677-2462.

Depending on their work load, it will take from 1-4 weeks to have your articles filed. As verification of your organization, a receipt for the filing will be returned to you.

If you're in a hurry, you can get faster service if you overnight or deliver the Articles yourself. Overnighted or hand-delivered filings are returned in 24-48 hours. If you send the Articles via an overnight service like FedEx, be sure to include a prepaid airbill so the Corporation Division can send the filed copy back to you.

If you need more information regarding this step, see page 90.

Step 3. Take Care of Organizational Matters

❏ *When the Articles return from the State, complete and adopt the "Operating Agreement" found on page 97. Keep it with your records.*

❏ *Issue member certificates to each member.*

In this step, all you have to do is complete and adopt the operating agreement on page 97, and issue a member Articles to each member. This is done after your articles have been filed with the state. Your operating agreement, meeting minutes and similar documents, are to be filed with the company records. Do not send these items to the state.

Securities registration...

Member certificates are considered a "security" like corporate stocks or bonds. If you sell an interest in your LLC to investors or others who will not take part in the day-to-day operations of the company, you may need to register your stock with the Securities Division of The Secretary of State's Office. Their telephone number is (317) 232-6681. If you have more questions about registering securities, call the State at the number above, and see page 34 of this book. Transactions are usually exempt from registration with the state if all the following conditions are met.

1. *The number of Indiana residents purchasing an ownership interest in the last 12 months is 20 or fewer, and*
2. *The sale or issuance is not offered in sales literature or advertised, and*
3. *Commission isn't paid to anyone for selling an interest in the company, and*
4. *The owners are purchasing the interest as an investment and not for resale.*

If you need more information regarding this step, see page 93.

Step 4. Prepare a Company Record Book

❏ *Prepare or purchase an LLC record book with a company seal.*

❏ *Organize your documents in the record book.*

❏ *Use the company seal to emboss the member certificates and Operating Agreement.*

❏ *After you've completed the steps above, take a look at Chapter 5 for a checklist of some things you'll need to do after forming your LLC.*

Properly maintained records are the only evidence of a properly formed and legally valid limited liability company. They are vital in preventing someone from winning a lawsuit against you by "piercing" your limited liability protection. Your records are probably the first thing the IRS will ask to see if you ever get audited. Also, bankers and investors will want to see your records if you seek financing for your business.

Most people use a customized limited liability company "outfit" or "kit" to organize their records. A customized outfit typically includes a seal engraved with the company name, color member certificates typeset with the company name, some handy meeting forms and a standard operating agreement, all separated by tabbed dividers and enclosed in a nice binder with the company name embossed in gold lettering on the spine. You can get an outfit at most legal stationery stores. If you can't find one locally, they are available from Consumer Publishing. See the brochure at the back of the book for information. If you need more information regarding this step, see page 94.

After completing these steps, be sure to review chapter five for a checklist of things every new business needs to do before commencing business - things like getting a business permit and a Federal Employer ID number.

PART THREE - FORMING A PARTNERSHIP

Of the three types of business organizations covered in this book, the process of forming a partnership is the simplest. Basically all you need to do when forming a partnership is choose a name and write a partnership agreement. There are no state filings, no Articles of Incorporation, etc. In summary:

Step 1. *Choose your partnership name.*
Step 2. *Write or adopt a partnership agreement.*
Step 3. *Take care of general business requirements.*

All you have to do to form a partnership in Indiana is complete the partnership agreement found on page 117, have each partner sign it, and give each partner a copy. A partnership agreement is an agreement between the partners that documents how the partners have agreed to operate the partnership. It dictates items like the responsibility and authority of each partner, how monies will be divided, and how ownership is divided. This agreement is not required to be written. It can be simply an oral understanding between the partners - but beware. An unwritten agreement is the making of a disagreement. It is best to have a written partnership agreement.

Organizing your partnership under one name and conducting business under another is known as using a "fictitious" or "assumed" name, or "doing business as" (dba). Using a fictitious name allows you to form your partnership using the names of the partners, and transact business under one or more descriptive names. Using a fictitious name, the partnership "Jones, Brown, Gray, and Smith" can conduct business under a more descriptive name like "Midtown Sandwich Shop."

To use a fictitious name, you'll need to file a "Certificate of Assumed Business Name" with the County Recorder for your county. The county filing fee varies by county. See your county recorder for more information.

ARTICLES OF INCORPORATION
STATE OF INDIANA

Pursuant to Indiana Business Corporation Law as amended, the undersigned individual submits these Articles of Incorporation for the purpose of forming a domestic for profit corporation.

1. The name of the Corporation is:

2. The street address of the corporation's initial registered office, and the name of its initial registered agent at that office are as follows:

3. The post office address of the corporation's principal office is:

4. The corporation is authorized to issue   shares of no par value, common stock, with identical rights and privileges, the transfer of which is restricted according to the Bylaws of the corporation.

5. This instrument was prepared by the incorporator. The name and street address of the corporation's sole incorporator is:

6. A Director of the corporation may not be held liable to the corporation or its shareholders for monetary damages due to a breach of fiduciary duty, unless the breach is a result of self-dealing, intentional misconduct, or illegal actions.

In witness whereof, the undersigned, being all the incorporators of the corporation named above, execute these Articles of Incorporation and verify, subject to penalties of perjury, that the statements contained herein are true.

Date:

Incorporator's Name:

Incorporator's Signature

INSTRUCTIONS
DO NOT RECORD THIS PAGE

1. Enter the name of the corporation. The corporate name must include one of the following: Incorporated, Corporation, Limited, Company or Inc., Corp., Ltd., or Co.

2. Enter the name and STREET address of the corporation's initial registered agent. You can serve as your corporation's own registered agent. Your home address is acceptable.

3. Enter the corporation's mailing address.

4. Enter the number of shares of stock that your corporation will be authorized to issue. You can authorize more shares than you plan to issue. There is no limit on the number of shares that you may have.

5. Enter your name and street address here. You're only required to have one incorporator.

6. This statement is included for your protection.

Complete the bottom of the form and have the incorporator sign the Articles of Incorporation with ink.

File by mail, overnight courier or in person:
Secretary of State
Division of Corporations
Room E018
Indianapolis, IN 46204

ARTICLES OF ORGANIZATION
STATE OF INDIANA

Pursuant to The Indiana Business Flexibility Act as amended, the undersigned individual submits these Articles of Organization for the purpose of forming a domestic limited liability company.

1. The name of the limited liability company is:

2. The street address of the limited liability company's initial registered office, and the name of its initial registered agent at that office are as follows:

3. The post office address of the limited liability company's principal office is:

4. The duration of the limited liability company is perpetual.

5. This instrument was prepared by the organizer. The name and street address of the limited liability company's sole organizer is:

6. The limited liability company will be member managed.

In witness whereof, the undersigned, being all the organizers of the limited liability company named above, execute these Articles of Organization and verify, subject to penalties of perjury, that the statements contained herein are true.

Date:

Organizer's Name:

Organizer's Signature

INSTRUCTIONS
DO NOT RECORD THIS PAGE

1. Enter the name of the company. The name must include one of the following: limited liability company, LLC or L.L.C.

2. Enter the name and STREET address of the company's initial registered agent. You can serve as your corporation's own registered agent. Your home address is acceptable.

3. Enter the company's mailing address.

4. This statement is required by law.

5. Enter your name and street address here. You're only required to have one organizer.

6. This statement is required by law.

Complete the bottom of the form and have the incorporator sign the Articles of Organization with ink.

File by mail, overnight courier or in person:
Secretary of State
Division of Corporations
Room E018
Indianapolis, IN 46204

Index

Corporate Supplies

STANDARD KIT:
An attractive, efficient 3-ring turned-edge binder. Available in black, tan green or black/burgundy.
(Black/burgundy additional)

ECONOLINE KIT:
A gold decorated vinyl binder, corporate name is printed on replaceable gold leaf spine insert. Available in black or brown.

HEAVY DUTY KIT:
A rugged, extra-strength 3-ring binder that is as attractive as it is durable. Binder is decorated in gold, and equipped with metal hinges for additional strength and security. Available in brown, black or green.

SEALS:
We offer a wide variety of desk and pocket seals, including corporate, notary and "From the Desk of…"

DELUXE KIT:
A luxurious, leather-like cover and classic rounded library spine, with triple-post binding to secure your documents. Available in black/burgundy or green.

CERTIFICATES:
Our company provides lithographed Over-The-Counter and American Stock Exchange certificates. We can supply certificates for every corporate need.

EACH KIT INCLUDES:

- Corporate name gold-stamped on spine
- Customized folding corporate seal with carry pouch
- 20 custom-printed, numbered stock certificates
- Time-saving **preprinted** minutes and bylaws **or** blank pages for minutes
- Stock Transfer Ledger
- Matching slipcase
- Special forms section including IRS requirements for Sub-Chapter S Filings, medical and dental reimbursement plans, and Section 1244 forms
- Specialized index dividers.

All kits may be ordered for Not-for-Profit, Close Corporations, LLCs, and Professional Corporations, with corresponding minutes and bylaws.

The Incorporating Without A Lawyer Series

Incorporating is a routine procedure that basically consists of putting your name and address on a standard form, holding a meeting, and issuing stock. Our books will show you the quickest and easiest way to incorporate your business in any of 33 states—including the popular state of Nevada. They'll lead you step-by-step through the incorporating process of either a C or an S corporation, and come complete with ready-to-use forms and genuine GOES® stock certificates.

Available States:

AL	AR	AZ	CA	CO	CT
DC	FL	GA	IL	IN	KS
KY	MA	MD	MI	MN	MO
MS	NC	NJ	NY	NV	OH
OK	OR	PA	TN	TX	UT
VA	WA	WI			

A Delaware book is also available. Please see *How to Form Your Own Corporation Without a Lawyer for Less Than $75* on page two.

—*incorporating made easy* $24.⁹⁵

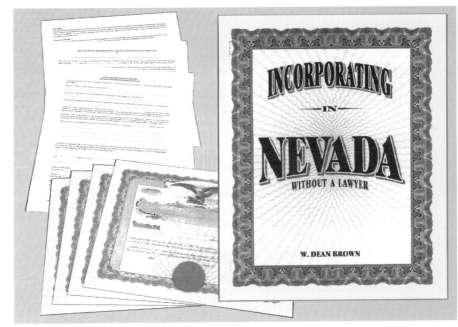

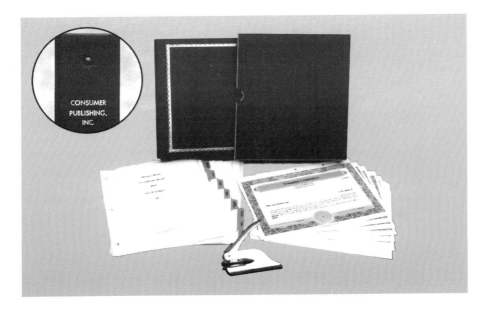

Standard Corporate Outfit

Well kept records are the sign of a properly organized corporation and can protect its legal status. To store your corporate records, we offer the finest corporate record books available. Personalized especially for you, this outfit features a sturdy, handsomely designed 3-ring binder with your corporate name embossed in gold on the spine. It is made from a rich, leather grained vinyl and comes with a matching slipcase.

Also included:

- A heavy duty, chrome–plated seal engraved with your corporate name, state and year of incorporation.

- 20 numbered stock certificates custom printed with the corporate name and a stock transfer ledger.

- Preprinted minutes and bylaws, medical & dental reimbursement plan, Subchapter S forms, Section 1244 forms, and annual meeting forms

—*O–ring binder in black, green, or tan* $63.⁰⁰
—*D–ring binder in black/burgundy combination* $68.⁰⁰

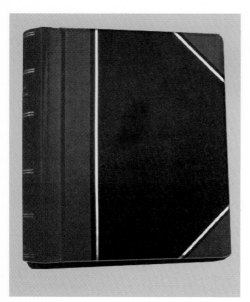

Deluxe Corporate Outfit

This beautiful outfit includes everything that our standard kit does with a deluxe black & burgundy binder that looks and feels like real leather. It features a rounded library spine–gold embossed with your corporate name, triple post binding and a matching slip case. It is also available in green or black–with a gold border on the front.

—all seals and outfits ship within 24 hours $89.⁰⁰

Leather Corporate Outfit

This beautiful outfit includes everything that our Deluxe kit does with a genuine leather binder.

—Available in black or burgundy. $199.⁰⁰

Seal Only

The same high quality chrome–plated corporate seal available with our kits is available alone. The seal is engraved with the name of your corporation, the state and date of incorporation.

—next day service is available $30.⁰⁰

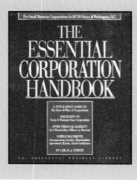

Taking Care of Your Corporation

shows you how to take care of day-to-day corporate business and comply with state law requirements for keeping corporate records. It explains how to hold corporate meetings, keep and prepare corporate minutes, pass board and shareholder resolutions, legally document corporate transactions, amend articles and bylaws, prepare buy/sell provisions to control the sale of corporate stock and more.

—for corporate secretaries. $26.⁹⁵

How to Form your Own Corporation w/o a Lawyer for Less Than $75

In its 20th edition, this book has incorporated more businesses than any other. If you want to incorporate in Delaware, this is the book for you. It has everything you need including the certificate of incorporation, minutes, bylaws and step-by-step instructions.

—the Delaware book $19.⁹⁵

The Essential Corporation Handbook

An "owner's manual" for your corporation, this book explains all the hows and whys of corporations. It covers everything from incorporating to dissolution. Subjects include—piercing of the corporate veil, shareholder buy/sell agreements, securities law, the roles of officers and directors, mergers, bylaws, proxies and more. It also includes checklists to properly form and maintain your corp.

—an owners manual for your corp. $19.⁹⁵

Stand Up To The IRS

is a hands on guide to battling the IRS and coaxing favorable decisions from agency personnel. It shows you how to defend yourself in an audit, challenge an incorrect tax bill, negotiate an installment plan, appeal an audit decision, file delinquent tax returns, support your deductions, and represent yourself in tax court. "Best personal finance book", says *Money Magazine*.

—a necessity for CPA's. $21.⁹⁵

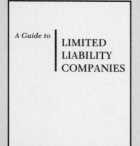

A Guide to Limited Liability Companies

provides a short but thorough discussion on this popular new form of business entity. It includes a historical overview, explores the formation and accounting, transferring interest, Federal and state tax treatment of LLC's and much more. It also compares LLC's with partnerships and Subchapter S corporations.

176 pages $29.⁹⁵

How to Form a Nonprofit Corporation

explains everything you need to know to start and operate a nonprofit corporation. A special appendix includes the specific requirements for incorporating your organization in your state. It also includes complete instructions for obtaining tax-exempt and public charity status with the IRS.

—instructions for all 50 states $39.⁹⁵

Plan Your Estate With a Living Trust

is simply the most comprehensive guide to estate planning available. It covers topics from basic planning to sophisticated tax saving strategies. It's the only book that shows you how to create an estate plan tailored to your needs. Good in all states except Louisiana. Includes durable powers of attorney, and living wills too!

—a complete handbook $24.⁹⁵

Business Owners Guide to Accounting & Bookkeeping

is a nontechnical, easy to understand book that will teach you the basics of accounting and how to keep your own books. Not only will it teach you how to prepare your own financial statements, but it'll also show you how to make them look their best for creditors.

—accounting made easy $19.⁹⁵

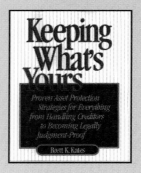

The Legal Guide for Starting & Running a Small Business

This book is a must-have comprehensive legal handbook for entrepreneurs. It covers all areas of operating a business including corporations, partnerships, business purchases, contracts, licenses, permits, leases, contractors, hiring & firing, customers, ind. contractors, insurance, taxes and more.

—your own desktop lawyer $24.⁹⁵

The Home Based Entrepreneur

This all new and fully updated edition covers everything you'll need to know to legally operate your business from home. This book will show you how to deal with zoning, labor laws, licenses & how to make the most of tax deductions for your home office.

—for home offices $19.⁹⁵

Keeping What's Yours

Today's lawsuit explosion makes every business person vulnerable to costly legal claims. This book is the insider's guide to asset protection and will show you how to legally and ethically protect yourself and your property from lawsuits. Among other strategies, it shows how to use your corporation and trusts to protect what's yours. The title says it all...

—protect your assets $19.⁹⁵

Starting & Operating a Business Series

is the best one-stop resource to *current* state and Federal regulations that affect your business. It'll help you cut through the red tape in your state and get you started off on the right foot. It includes extensive checklists and information on permits, licenses, business taxes, insurance, employees, payroll & unemployment taxes, workers comp., and more.

—please specify state $24.⁹⁵

Trademark—How to Name Your Business & Product

is by far the best comprehensive do-it-yourself trademark book available—a user friendly guide to the laws that govern commercial names. This book will show you how to choose a name competitors can't copy, conduct a trademark search, register your trademark with the U.S. Patent and Trademark office, protect your trademark from infringement and more.

—protect your name $29.⁹⁵

Patent it Yourself

contains all the forms and specific step–by–step instructions that you'll need to patent your invention in the United States. It explains the entire process from the patent search to the actual application. It also covers use and licensing, marketing of your invention and how to deal with infringement.

—save a small fortune $39.⁹⁵

The Employer's Legal Handbook

This is the most comprehensive resource available that covers your questions about hiring, firing, and everything in between. Its 350 pages include topics like—discrimination, privacy rights, employee rights, workplace health and safety, employee benefits, wages, hours, tips and commissions, sexual harassment, termination, taxes, liability insurance, and safe hiring practices.

—stay out of court $29.⁹⁵

How to Write a Business Plan

Your banker, investors, and the Small Business Administration need your business plan, but where do you start? Used by SBA offices around the country, this 272 page best-seller comes complete with examples, forms, and work sheets that show you how to write a winning business plan in only *one* day. It will help you present your business opportunity to bankers and investors in a format they'll understand.

—finish your business plan in a day $19.⁹⁵

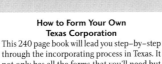

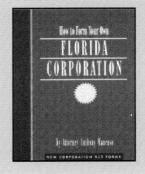

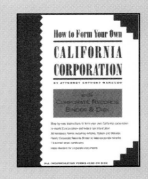

How to Form Your Own New York Corporation

This 272 page book will lead you step–by–step through the incorporating process in New York. Not only does it have everything you'll need, but the forms are also included on a DOS 3 1/2" disk.

Book, and disk $39.⁹⁵

How to Form Your Own Texas Corporation

This 240 page book will lead you step–by–step through the incorporating process in Texas. It not only has all the forms that you'll need but also includes the forms on a DOS 3 1/2" disk.

Book, and disk $39.⁹⁵

How to Form Your Own Florida Corporation

This 225 page book will lead you step–by–step through the incorporating process in Florida. Not only does it have everything you'll need, but the forms are also included on a 3 1/2" DOS disk.

Book, and disk $39.⁹⁵

How to Form Your Own California Corporation

includes a 288 page step-by-step incorporating guide and a 3.5" IBM disk with all the forms you'll need. Included to keep your corporate papers organized is a corporate records binder that includes 10 stock certificates, and indexed dividers.

Binder, book & disk $39.⁹⁵

Order Form

ORDERING OPTIONS

1. *Call* us at 1-800-677-2462 and place your order using a Visa or MasterCard.

2. *Fax* your order, credit card number and expiration date to 1-423-539-6600

3. *Mail* your order with a personal check, business check, money order or credit card information to:

Consumer Publishing, Inc.
P.O. Box 23830
Concord, TN 37933-1830

RETURNS

Your satisfaction is guaranteed. We only ask that books be returned in saleable condition within 30 days. Software must be unopened.

SHIP TO:

_____
name

_____
address

_____
suite or unit number

_____
city   state   zip

_____
area code & telephone number — in case we have a question

Credit Card Orders:

_____
name on card

_____
card number   exp. (month/year)

_____
signature

SHIPPING OPTIONS

Books–We ship books via U.S. Priority Mail unless you need overnight delivery.

Priority Mail arrives in 2-3 days and costs $3 for the first book and $1 for each additional book.

Federal Express arrives the next day and charges depend on the weight of the book(s). Please call for Fed Ex rates.

Corporate outfits and seals are shipped within 24 hours by UPS unless you request overnight delivery. Overnight orders must be placed before 2 pm Eastern time.

The UPS charge is $4 per item. Overnight delivery via Airborne Express is $9 per item. *A street address is required for delivery of corporate outfits and seals.*

Books & Software

Quant.	Description		Price Ea.	Total
	A Guide to Limited Liability Companies		29.95	
	Business Owners Guide to Accounting and Bookkeeping		19.95	
	How to Form a Nonprofit Corporation		39.95	
	How to Form Your Own Corporation w/o a Lawyer for Less than $75—Delaware		19.95	
	How to Form Your Own CALIFORNIA Corporation—book, binder and DOS 3.5 inch disk.		39.95	
	How to Form Your Own NEW YORK Corporation—book, and DOS 3.5 inch disk.		39.95	
	How to Form Your Own TEXAS Corporation—book, and DOS 3.5 inch disk.		39.95	
	How to Form Your Own FLORIDA Corporation—book, and DOS 3.5 inch disk.		39.95	
	How to Write a Business Plan		19.95	
	Keeping What's Yours		19.95	
	Patent it Yourself		39.95	
	Plan Your Estate With a Living Trust		24.95	
	Stand Up to the IRS		21.95	
	Starting & Operating a Business Series	— *specify state(s):*	24.95	
	Taking Care of Your Corporation		26.95	
	The Employer's Legal Handbook		29.95	
	The Essential Corporation Handbook		19.95	
	The Home Based Entrepreneur		19.95	
	The Incorporating Without a Lawyer series	— *specify state(s):*	24.95	
	The Legal Guide for Starting and Running a Small Business		24.95	
	Trademark, How to Name Your Business & Product		29.95	
	Blank Stock Certificates—specify gold, green, or blue	package of 10 certificates	5.00	

Corporate Supplies

Quant.	Description					Price Ea.	Total
	Standard Corporate Outfit	—*circle color*	black	tan (camel)	green	63.00	
	Standard Corporate Outfit—D ring binder in black/burgundy					68.00	
	Deluxe Corporate Outfit	—*circle color*	black/burg.	black	green	89.00	
	Leather Corporate outfit					199.00	
	Seal Only					30.00	

Prices are current as of 11/1/95, and may be subject to change.

Corporate Information

_____
corporate name as it will appear on the outfit — either ALL CAPS – Initial Caps – or any combination of caps and lower case letters.

_____
date of inc.   state of inc.   number of AUTHORIZED shares   par value   is it common stock ?

Subtotal _____
(TN residents only) Sales tax _____
Shipping _____
Total _____